PEACE LIKE A SPIDER

and Other Devotions for Teens

PEACE LIKE A SPIDER

and Other Devotions for Teens

KARL HAFFNER

REVIEW AND HERALD® PUBLISHING ASSOCIATION
HAGERSTOWN, MD 21740

Unless otherwise noted, Bible texts in this book are from the *Holy Bible, New
International Version.* Copyright © 1973, 1978, 1984, International Bible Society.
Used by permission of Zondervan Bible Publishers.

Verses marked TLB are taken from *The Living Bible,* copyright © 1971 by
Tyndale House Publishers, Wheaton, Ill. Used by permission.

This book was
Edited by Gerald Wheeler
Designed by Patricia S. Wegh
Cover illustration by Bruce Day
Typeset: Palatino 10.5/12

PRINTED IN U.S.A.

98 97 96 95 94   10 9 8 7 6 5 4 3 2

R&H Cataloging Service
Haffner, Karl Mark, 1961-
    Peace like a spider and other teen devotionals.

    1. Teenagers—Prayer books and devotions—
English.   I. Title.
                242.63

ISBN 0-8280-0888-4

Dedication

DEDICATED TO MY WIFE, CHERIÉ

Whether it's scrunching into a birthday present . . .

or snapping pictures of a Hershey bomb . . .

or an escort to the deck of Festivale . . .

you punctuate life with surprise.

. . . Here's one more.

HAPPY BIRTHDAY!

CONTENTS

THE FOUNDATION OF SUCCESS

FEELING SUCCESS

SUCCEEDING IN RELATIONSHIPS

SUCCEEDING IN THE TOUGH BATTLES

SPIRITUAL SUCCESS

SUCCESS: WHAT DOES IT MEAN?

The Foundation of Success

PASSION

Passion. What comes to your mind when you hear the word? Steamy perfume commercials? A Jesse Jackson speech on equality? An Olympic athlete skating for gold? What is your picture of passion?

Everyone has a passion. For some it's animal rights. For others it's money. For many it's nothing more than television reruns. Or romance novels. Or Mountain Dew and pizza.

For Hideaki Tomoyori, of Yokohama, Japan, it's *pi*—which he recited from memory to 40,000 places in 17 hours and 21 minutes.

To Reg Mellor, passion means "ferret legging." At age 72 he is the reigning world champion of ferret legging—a contest in which competitors tie their trousers at the ankles and subsequently insert into those trousers a couple particularly vicious, fur-coated, foot-long carnivores called ferrets. The brave contestants' belts are then pulled tight, and they proceed to stand in front of the judges as long as they can while these animals, with claws like hypodermic needles and teeth like number 16 carpet tacks, try to get out. Reg Mellor holds the world record at five hours and 26 minutes.

Henrietta Howland Green equated passion with money. Although she kept a balance of more than $31 million in one bank alone, she was so stingy that her son had to have his leg amputated because of the delays in finding a *free* medical clinic. As for herself, she lived off cold oatmeal because she was too thrifty to heat it. Her estate totaled more than $95 million.

Everyone has a passion for something. So what is your passion? What is so important that you will invest your life in pursuit of it? What keeps you awake at night? What do you cry about? What consumes your time and energy?

Hans Küng, the Roman Catholic theologian, writes this about

passion: "We all have a personal god—a supreme value by which we regulate everything, to which we orientate ourselves, for which if need be we will sacrifice everything. And if this is not the true God, then it is some kind of an idol, an old or a new one. Money, career, sex, pleasure—none of them evil things in themselves but enslaving for those to whom they become god."

Choose your passion carefully. For passion is the spark plug that ignites action. And action exposes your god.

"O GOD, YOU ARE MY GOD, EARNESTLY I SEEK YOU; MY SOUL THIRSTS FOR YOU, MY BODY LONGS FOR YOU, IN A DRY AND WEARY LAND WHERE THERE IS NO WATER" (PSALM 63:1).

INTEGRITY

$50,000 WORTH OF INTEGRITY

The headline could have proclaimed "Tonya Harding Becomes Pope," and I would have been less shocked. I stared at the front page of the Seattle *Times* in disbelief.

"Snohomish, Washington—Lisa Thorpe of Lynnwood passed the good Samaritan test Sunday when she found $50,000 cash in a roadside ditch—and gave it to police.

"According to Snohomish County sheriff's spokesman Elliot Woodal, a Snohomish man, 65, withdrew the cash Saturday, planning to deposit it in another bank. But first the man, who recently had a death in his family, drove home and became distracted, leaving the money bag on the running board of his pickup truck. Later he drove the truck on an errand and didn't realize until early Sunday that the money was missing.

"Thorpe was on a Sunday drive with her family when she noticed a money clip and money on the road in the 200 block of

Dubuque Road north of Snohomish. When she stopped to investigate, she found the bag of cash in the ditch. Deputies traced the money through papers in the bag."

The story hit me like an avalanche of rocks. Coincidentally, I had driven on the 200 block of Dubuque Road that Sunday and had whizzed by $50,000! The question still taunts me: "What would I have done with the money?"

Captivated by the story, I set out to contact Lisa Thorpe. Fifteen phone calls and an hour of frustration later I had Lisa on the line. "Hi, um, Lisa?" I stammered. "You, ah, don't know me, but I read about what you did last week, um, with the $50,000 and all, and I want you to know I find your story very inspiring."

"Thank you," she replied modestly. "I appreciate the call."

"Um, one question," I blurted out before she could hang up. I had to ask the burning question. "Were you tempted to keep the money?"

"No, not really."

"Why not?"

"Well," she said, "you may not understand, but have you ever heard of the Ten Commandments?"

What Seventh-day Adventist minister hasn't heard of the Ten Commandments? A fourth generation Adventist, I could recite the Ten Commandments before I could say my full name. As a loyal Adventist I have my $10 bill and my Ten Commandments, and I won't break either one of them.

"Yes," I assured her, "I've heard of the Ten Commandments."

"Then you know about the one that says not to steal?"

"Yep."

"Then you know why I . . ."

"Yes, I know."

Her final words before our goodbyes cut like a surgeon's scalpel: "My integrity is worth far more than $50,000."

What about you? What is your integrity worth?

Integrity is the primary ingredient of a successful life. It is the cornerstone in the foundation of success—living honestly when no one's watching.

You can drive a Corvette, get a degree from Harvard, vacation in Australia, golf with an even handicap, and sing like Barbra Streisand, but you'll never be truly successful unless everything you do is undergirded with integrity. Only when truthfulness is deeply embedded in your character will you taste the heady potion of success.

So what is your integrity worth?

"BUT JUST AS HE WHO CALLED YOU IS HOLY, SO BE HOLY IN ALL YOU DO; FOR IT IS WRITTEN: 'BE HOLY, BECAUSE I AM HOLY'" (1 PETER 1:15, 16).

TRUST

WHOM DO YOU TRUST?

Which news source do you trust most? least?

A Gallup survey asked more than 2,000 adults to tell what they considered the most trustworthy news source. Guess their responses by rating the most trustworthy source (number 1) to the least trustworthy (number 10). After completing the quiz, refer to the key. Give yourself a point for every one you guessed in the right order.

___ *Reader's Digest*	___ Geraldo Rivera
___ *USA Today*	___ *National Enquirer*
___ Ted Koppel	___ Barbara Walters
___ Walter Cronkite	___ *Wall Street Journal*
___ Phil Donahue	___ Dan Rather

How did you do? Whom do you trust to report the news honestly? On what basis do you base that trust?

Did any of the results surprise you? Why?

"Trust Me"

Every day we make decisions based on trust. We expect the newscaster to report honest news. We assume the bus driver will drive safely. We have faith the teacher will provide accurate information. We count on drivers to abide by the traffic rules as we amble down the sidewalk. We have confidence that our parents will give good advice. The choices we make are based on trust.

Good decisions rest on good information. And good information comes from those we trust to give it to us.

So whom do you trust?

MTV?

Your friends? Beavis and, uh, his sidekick?

Your teachers?

God?

Who influences you most when you make decisions?

Do You Trust God?

The Bible is full of stories of men and women whose lives changed when they chose to trust God. Peter switched professions. Nicodemus shifted priorities. Mary Magdalene transformed her lifestyle.

The cripple at the pool of Bethesda acquired a new mode of transportation when Jesus said to stand up and walk. Because the man trusted Jesus, he stood. And for the first time in 38 years he walked!

Wouldn't you find it exhilarating to do the same? to stand when Jesus says stand? to trust Him completely?

When Jesus says you're forgiven, to unload the guilt?

When Jesus says He'll take care of you, to stop worrying?

When Jesus says you are saved, to bury your fears?

When Jesus says you are a child of the King, to act like it?

So when Jesus says to stand, why not stand?

I love the story of the private who captured the runaway horse of Napoleon. When he returned the animal, Napoleon said, "Thank you, Captain."

With one word the private became a captain. And he believed it. He wore a new uniform and ate his next meal at the officers' table and moved out of his barracks into the officers' quarters. Because Napoleon said it, he believed it.

Why not live the same way?

"TRUST IN THE LORD WITH ALL YOUR HEART AND LEAN NOT ON

YOUR OWN UNDERSTANDING; IN ALL YOUR WAYS ACKNOWLEDGE HIM, AND HE WILL MAKE YOUR PATHS STRAIGHT" (PROV. 3:5, 6).

Key to news source quiz: 1. Walter Cronkite, 2. Ted Koppel, 3. *The Wall Street Journal,* 4. Dan Rather, 5. *Reader's Digest,* 6. Barbara Walters, 7. Geraldo Rivera, 8. *USA Today,* 9. Phil Donahue, 10. *National Enquirer.*

VISION

A BIG (MAC) VISION

Perhaps few people have described the power of pursuing a compelling vision better than the late Ray Kroc. His vision ignited at a drive-in restaurant owned by the McDonald brothers in southern California. Intrigued by their mechanized approach to delivering a limited selection of foods quickly, Kroc studied the business and discussed expansion possibilities with the McDonald family. After some planning he entered into a partnership with the McDonalds in 1954.

Kroc recalled the excitement of changing his career in pursuit of a new vision: "When I flew back to Chicago that day, I had a freshly signed contract with the McDonald brothers in my briefcase. I was a battle-scarred veteran of business wars, but I was still eager to go into action. I was 52 years old. I had diabetes and incipient arthritis. I had lost my gallbladder and most of my thyroid gland in earlier campaigns. But I was convinced that the best was ahead of me. I was flying along at an altitude slightly higher than that of the plane."* From the outset, the vision felt right to Kroc.

The story, however, was not all milk shakes and hot-fudge sundaes. Bitter fights with the McDonalds, a variety of lawsuits,

---

*Ray Kroc, *Grinding It Out* (Washington, D.C.: Regnery Gateway Inc., 1977), p. 13.

and other harrowing experiences paved the road to fortune with bumps and potholes. Yet Kroc maintained that he was able to persevere because his vision for the fast-food business fueled him past the obstacles. He pressed through periods in which he doubted his employees, suppliers, lawyers, and even his family, but Kroc remained convinced that if he tenaciously pursued his vision, he could create a better future. From a corporate perspective, he did just that.

And from a biblical perspective, God has always used visionaries to alter the world. The apostle Paul found himself driven to fulfill a vision for ministry that God had entrusted to him. In the book of Acts we see the apostle preaching, teaching, and planting churches with a fervor missing from anyone who's working only for a paycheck. Rather, he worked tirelessly through beatings, shipwrecks, and prison sentences because he clearly saw God's vision for a better world.

Nehemiah accepted responsibility for rebuilding the walls of Jerusalem. Scripture tells us that for several days he couldn't sleep or eat or function because of the burning vision that consumed his life. His gutsy confrontations with opponents testified to the vision God had given him. Rather than collapsing under the pressure, Nehemiah stood firm on the basis of that vision—the very work that "my God had put in my heart to do for Jerusalem" (Neh. 2:12).

Moses received a clear vision from God to make a difference. Pursuing that vision meant 40 years of camping in the hot desert, leading an unruly band of whiners through times of sacrifice and pain. But driven by God's vision, Moses stuck with it.

God still calls people to pursue His vision for a better world. What vision has God given you?

"WHERE THERE IS NO VISION, THE PEOPLE PERISH"
(PROV. 29:18, KJV).

GENEROSITY

THE STICKY NICKEL

"Take that seat over there," the kid ordered as I walked into the barbershop.

I obeyed for two reasons. First, because there was only one seat in the crowded barbershop. (I should have expected as much, since it was the day after Thanksgiving.) Second, because the kid was adorable (especially with the cherry slobber dripping down his chin as he sucked a lollipop the size of a compact disc).

Freckles polka-dotted his face, his eyes sparkled with mischief, his dimples sank deep into his cheeks, and his mouth never stopped.

"I like turkey; do you like turkey?" he asked of anyone in the shop who cared to respond. "Daddy makes a good turkey, don't you, Dad? I can't wait till Christmas. Tomorrow we're going to see the Sonics play, ain't we, Dad? Sorry, sir, you have to stand until somebody leaves . . ."

Although I had brought a book to read, I found the boy's comments more interesting. I laughed at his childish ramblings.

After his haircut he turned to the hairstylist and complimented, "Thank you! I love my new haircut. It looks good on me!" He started out the door, then paused, marched back to the stylist, and exclaimed, "Oh, I almost forgot! Here, this is for you."

He fished from his pocket a nickel and handed it to the grinning stylist. She snatched the coin from his sticky little cherry-flavored fist.

When it was my turn for the barber's seat, I commented to the stylist, "He was a cute kid, wasn't he?"

"Yes," she agreed, "he sure was." After a pause she added, "He gave me my biggest tip of the day."

Her biggest tip? On the busiest day of the year, her biggest tip was a lousy cherry-slobbered nickel? Was that what she was telling me?

Of course not. I understood clearly.

The nickel was not valuable because of the size of the gift, but rather because of the heart of the giver. Attitude and motive are always more important than amount. Furthermore, once a person cultivates a taste for generous giving, the amount becomes immaterial.

So we return our paltry nickels to God:

- an hour to help the neighbor shovel the snow out of her driveway.
- a dollar in the red bucket outside of K Mart at Christmas time.
- a kind word.
- a smile.
- a flower to Aunt Etna in the nursing home.

Each is a paltry nickel that brings a smile to the face of God when it comes from the innocent heart of His child. For God is not concerned with the size of our gift but with the heart of the giver.

"FOR GOD LOVES A CHEERFUL GIVER" (2 COR. 9:7).

HARD WORK

THE COMMON TRAIT OF ALL SUCCESSFUL PEOPLE

George and Alec Gallup, the famous public opinion pollsters, completed some of the most extensive research on the qualities of success. The two men invested thousands of hours interviewing successful people in search of the common factors among all of them.

Talking with high achievers in business, the arts, literature, religion, the military, and so on, they asked questions about family background, personality, hobbies, personal values, and education. The results of their research they published in a book called *The Great American Success Story*.

The common denominator among the thousands of successful people was not extraordinary talent, or lucky breaks, or wealth. It was much simpler. Hard work. It almost seems too simple, doesn't it? Hard work!

While their answers varied widely, one common thread weaved consistently through the stories: success wasn't something that just happened. Rather, they made it happen through focused effort and dogged determination. No shortcuts. No simple ride. No magic. No tricks. No secrets.

Success came to those willing to pay the price of hard work. The harvest of success had a direct relationship to the seeds of hard work planted. The researchers concluded: "So what we have here is an affirmation of the old-fashioned American credo that hard work and determination pay off."

Hal Sherbeck is a well-known coach who produced winning teams at Missoula High School, the University of Montana, and Fullerton Community College. A reporter for the Los Angeles *Times* asked him, "What's the secret of your success?"

Without hesitation Sherbeck quoted this poem as the credo of his life:

> Press on.
> Nothing in the world
> Can take the place of persistence.
> Talent will not;
> Nothing is more common
> Than unsuccessful men
> With talent.
> Genius will not;
> Unrewarded genius
> Is almost a proverb.
> Education will not;

The world is full of
Educated derelicts.
Persistence and determination
Alone are important.*

Coach Sherbeck offered no simple secret for success—just a commitment to hard work.

"REMEMBER THIS: WHOEVER SOWS SPARINGLY WILL ALSO REAP SPARINGLY, AND WHOEVER SOWS GENEROUSLY WILL ALSO REAP GENEROUSLY" (2 COR. 9:6).

---

* Author unknown.

DELAYED GRATIFICATION

THE VALUE OF THE DESERT

A parent once approached a college president and asked, "How long will it take you to educate my son?"

"That all depends on what you want your son to become," the administrator replied. "It takes nature two weeks to grow a squash, but 100 years to grow an oak."

What do you want to become? A squash? Or an oak? Your ability to wait determines your destiny. To delay pleasure, to pay now and play later, will bring great rewards.

But waiting is hard to do in a society that worships comfort, ease, pleasure, and instant gratification. Russian comedian Yakov Smirnoff observes: "Coming from the Soviet Union, I was not prepared for the incredible variety of products available in American grocery stores. I couldn't believe all the wonderful things they have. On my first shopping trip I saw powdered milk

. . . you just add water, and you get milk. Then I saw powdered orange juice . . . you just add water, and you get orange juice. And then I saw baby powder . . . I thought to myself, *What a country!*" *

We crave slick, quick, "just add water" solutions to all problems, don't we? It's the American way. Play now, pay later. The commercial shouts: "Master the possibilities!" Advertisers splash enticing pictures of all the things you can have and the exotic places you can explore just by saying "Charge it!" Play now—pay later.

While the majority bank on this philosophy, the minority who will experience true success will ignore the shortcut and opt for the long, risky road. The *only* pathway to success.

One of the most meaningful Jewish celebrations is the Feast of Sukkot. It commemorates the 40 years the Jews spent wandering in the wilderness. Although it was only 200 miles from Egypt to Canaan, it took God's people 40 years to make the trip! The trek should have taken no longer than a couple weeks.

The Feast of Sukkot reminds the Jews of the value of meandering in the desert. It was during this time when the Israelites received the Ten Commandments and the pattern for the tabernacle. In the wilderness a new generation emerged, ready to enter the Promised Land.

The most significant kinds of growth cannot be hurried. A nation of slaves needs longer than two weeks to be transformed into a nation of free people. A young man needs longer than a few years to develop a deep abiding trust in God. A young woman needs time to paint a masterpiece. Great accomplishments grow out of wilderness experiences.

It's the long road. It's humid. And uncomfortable. And hot. It requires determination. And perseverance. And focus.

But it is the only pathway to success.

As Charles Malik, a former president of the United Nations General Assembly, once said, "I am not foolish enough to believe that today or tomorrow the world is going to be radically changed. There is no shortcut to heaven except through the healing influence of Jesus Christ."†

---

*Yakov Smirnoff, *America on Six Rubles a Day* (New York: Random House, Inc., 1987), p. 51.
†Houston *Post*, Apr. 11, 1969.

Spiritual success. Financial success. Educational success. "There is no shortcut."

"SO GOD LED THE PEOPLE AROUND BY THE DESERT ROAD" (Ex. 13:18).

PERSEVERANCE

DOUGHNUTS, PIZZAS, AND ROSES

My freshman year in college was an education in itself. My buddy Steve and I learned a little about biology. A little about psychology. And a lot about life.

One of the most valuable lessons came on a Saturday night when we didn't have dates (which could have referred to almost every Saturday night). Instead, we went to Chattanooga to meet people. We met Rosita at Dunkin' Donuts, chatted with Bob at Bob's Coffee and Donuts, and spent a few minutes with Donna at The Donut Hole.

Much to our delight, we made an amazing discovery that evening—with a mixture of charm and coaxing, our new friends were willing to give us doughnuts—free!

By 11:30 that evening we had a dozen lemon-filled, a half-dozen chocolate cremes, a dozen bear claws, and an arsenal of other sugar bombs to share with the guys in the dorm.

The next Saturday night we also didn't have dates. (You're beginning to understand why, aren't you?) Sitting in my dorm room, Steve said, "You know, I've been thinking. If it works for doughnuts, why wouldn't it work for pizza?"

Faster than we could say cheese, we were racing toward the Pizza Hut on Third and Madison. We sauntered into the restaurant like Great Danes at a poodle convention.

"Smoking or non?" the cheery host greeted.

"We need to speak to the manager," I said.

The manager came to the counter. "How may I help you, gentlemen?"

"We were wondering, sir," Steve said tentatively, "if, um, you had some free pizzas sitting around. See, we're college kids with no money, no dates, and lots of time, so we thought you might like to help us out. Betty, our old '79 Datsun, knows we're broke, but she pulled into your parking lot anyway, so we thought we'd ask. What do you say?"

By now the manager was smiling. "Sure, what kind do you want?"

"Everything vegetarian except pineapple," I replied. "And since you're at it, could you throw in a couple cans of Sprite?"

The evening flew by as we collected free pizzas and pop around town!

The next Saturday night we had dates. (Scary, isn't it?) Intent on showering them with the finest amenities, we crashed a flower shop that week and went to work.

"We're a couple poor freshmen," I started, "and have dates this weekend. We'd love to give our dates some corsages. Any chance you'd be willing to donate to a worthy cause?"

The pudgy lady behind the counter looked like a red smiley face. "Sure!" she gleamed. "You boys remind me of my grandson. That's something he'd do."

The following Saturday night our dates looked fabulous sporting their five-rose corsages. I would argue they were the classiest ladies in the whole bowling alley!

Lounging around the room the following week, I wondered how far we could take our discovery. "If it works for doughnuts . . ." I mused.

"Yeah," Steve replied.

". . . and pizzas . . ."

"Yeah."

" . . . and flowers . . ."

"Yeah."

". . . why wouldn't it work at the Honda dealer?"

The more we thought about it, the more we liked the idea. So we made our way to the dealership and requested a couple

Honda XL250R motorcycles.

That experience taught us two valuable lessons. First, you don't get a free motorcycle unless you ask. Second, you don't get a free motorcycle even if you do ask (the Honda dealer looked as if we had asked him to bike to Mars), because anything worthwhile in life you have to pay for.

Count on it. Career success, financial gain, athletic skills, worthwhile relationships, educational accomplishment—anything worthwhile in life you have to pay for.

Too many people settle for the doughnuts and pizzas and flowers in life because they are unwilling to pay the price for whatever is truly valuable.

Want to enjoy the exhilaration of life's finest pleasures? Determine to pay the price, because nothing worthwhile comes free. Nothing.

"ALL HARD WORK BRINGS A PROFIT, BUT MERE TALK LEADS ONLY TO POVERTY" (PROV. 14:23).

CREATIVITY

WE'RE ALL FRENCH

Someone once said, "Being creative is like being French—either you are, or you aren't."

Maybe. Maybe not.

I have yet to meet a child who is not bursting with creativity.

Six-year-old Shannon gapes at the starry sky. "I'd like to eat a vanilla-chip cookie that big!"

When I was a little boy I'd sprawl over the grassy carpet and gaze at the floating clouds.

"What's that cloud?" Dad would quiz.

"That's a John Deere tractor," I would respond confidently. My answers were always right.

"How about that big cloud?"

"That's an explosion in a snow factory!"

How do we lose that fresh spirit? Why does rigor mortis of the brain begin at the end of childhood? Or to paraphrase Marilyn Ferguson in her book *The Aquarian Conspiracy* (J. P. Tarcher), "Why do human beings start out as butterflies and end up in cocoons?"

Let's face it. From the first grade we've been programmed to look for a single "right" answer to questions. Our teachers drilled us to *converge* on one solution rather than to *diverge* and explore the infinite possibilities. Thus we become convergent rather than divergent thinkers.

Research has indicated that 84 percent of a 5-year-old's thinking is divergent. But by second grade he or she uses divergent thinking only 10 percent of the time. And by age 45 only a scant 2 percent of a person's thinking is divergent.

Picasso battled convergent thinking. "I used to draw like Raphael," he said. "It has taken me a whole lifetime to learn to draw like a child." Oh, for the creativity of a child.

Paul MacCready, the prize-winning inventor of human- and solar-powered aircraft, recently shared with an audience at Yale what he considered to be the source of his success: "My secret weapon was complete naïveté. The experts' extra knowledge made them have blinders on." Oh, for the naïveté of a child!

Kids aren't afraid to ask dumb—or what we might think as dumb—questions. "Daddy, can I see the picture you just took of me?"

"No, sweetie, I have to take it to the store to have the film developed."

"But I want to see it now. Why can't you show me now?"

"Because."

"Because why?"

Several years ago these "dumb" questions led "sweetie's" father, Edwin Land, to invent the Polaroid camera. Oh, for the courage to ask the dumb questions of a child.

Open Your Mouth and Say "And"

Jung believed creative growth to be a process of reconciling

28

opposites. Either loving or hating your parents. Going with the guys for doughnuts or studying for a test.

Creativity combines opposites. It replaces "either/or" with "and." In divergent thinking, creativity allows all options.

Jesus loved to speak of paradoxes. "*Blessed* are they which are *persecuted*" (Matt. 5:10, KJV). "He that *findeth* his life shall *lose* it: and he that *loseth* his life for my sake shall *find* it" (Matt. 10:39, KJV).

Salvation is a paradox too. Jesus said, "Be ye therefore perfect, even as your Father which is in heaven is perfect" (Matt. 5:48, KJV). I read that and mumble, "I'll never make it to heaven."

Then I see "Believe on the Lord Jesus Christ, and thou shalt be saved" (Acts 16:31). "Now, that I can do!" I tell myself.

Enter creativity. Divergent, creative thinking will help you understand not only your world but also the gospel of Jesus better.

Jesus tells us how to be creative and harmonize opposites. "Unless you . . . become like little children, you will never enter the kingdom of heaven" (Matt. 18:3).

There's a little boy or girl inside of all of us. In a sense, we're all French.

PERSPECTIVE

CHANGE YOUR SEEING TO CHANGE YOUR SCENE

A college freshman wrote the following letter:
"Dear Mother,
"Since I have been away to college for a full semester, I think it is about time I bring you up-to-date about what is going on.

Shortly after I arrived at college, I got bored with dormitory life, so I stole $10 out of my roommate's purse. With the money I rented a mountain bike and crashed it into a telephone pole a few blocks from college. I broke my leg, but was rescued by the young doctor who lives upstairs in the apartment house on the corner. He took me in, set my leg, nursed me back to health, and thanks to him, I am hobbling around again. We wanted to let you know we are going to be married as soon as possible. Except we're having some trouble on the blood test because a disease keeps showing up. We do hope, however, we will be married before the baby arrives. And we'll be home shortly thereafter to live with you and Dad. I know that you will love the baby as much as you have me, even though we are both of a different religion. Please try to understand, the reason we are needing to come home and stay is because my doctor friend is wanting out of medical school.

"Really, Mom, I didn't steal $10 from my roommate, or rent a mountain bike, or hit a telephone pole, or break my leg. I did not meet a young doctor of a different religion, nor are we going to be married. There is no disease, or test, or baby to worry about. I won't be home to live, and he won't be either.

"I am, however, getting a D in geometry and an F in geology, and I wanted you to accept these grades in their proper perspective!"

It all depends on your perspective, doesn't it? Research conducted at Harvard University bears this out. It revealed that attitude is far more important than intelligence, education, special talent, or luck. The researchers concluded that up to 85 percent of success in life is a result of our perspective and how we interpret things. Only 15 percent comes from ability. Our attitude—that is, the perspective from which we choose to see things—is a crucial ingredient in the formula of success. As John Homer Miller said: "Your living is determined not so much by what life brings to you as by the attitude you bring to life; not so much by what happens to you as by the way your mind looks at what happens."

So how does your mind interpret the events in your life? How do you see things? What's your perspective?

Remind yourself to put things in the proper perspective the next time you get turned down for a date, or the pimple doesn't respond to a gallon of Clearasil, or a friend slam-dunks you by fueling a nasty rumor. See these irritations of life in the proper perspective. Change your seeing to change your scene!

"FOR AS HE THINKETH IN HIS HEART, SO IS HE"
(PROV. 23:7, KJV).

Feeling
Success

2

PEACE

WHEN PEACE LIKE A SPIDER

When Mark Twain was a young man, he worked as an editor and publisher of a growing newspaper in a small Missouri town. One day he received a letter from one of his subscribers. The subscriber said that he had found a spider in that morning's edition of his paper. He wanted to know if it was an omen of good luck or of bad luck.

Mark Twain, a hustling salesman as well as an editor, wrote his customer: "Dear Sir: Finding the spider in your newspaper yesterday morning was neither good luck nor bad luck for you. The spider was merely looking over our paper to see which of the town's merchants is not advertising. It will then go to that store, spin its web across the door, and live a life of undisturbed peace."

Sounds inviting, doesn't it? Who isn't looking for "a life of undisturbed peace"? Peace when your parents divorce. Peace when your grandma battles cancer. Peace when your girlfriend dumps you.

Evelyn Underhill once said, "It is God's will for us that we should possess an interior castle, against which the storms of life may beat without being able to disturb the serene quiet within; a spiritual life so firm and so serene that nothing can overthrow it."

You can discover this castle of peace. It doesn't mean you will enjoy freedom from all problems. But despite the problems, you can still have peace.

How? Only through the indwelling Prince of peace.

"YOU WILL KEEP IN PERFECT PEACE HIM WHOSE MIND IS STEADFAST, BECAUSE HE TRUSTS IN YOU" (ISA. 26:3).

JOY

THE "CHRISTIAN" WHO GROWLS

Have you ever known a spirit-filled grouch? Actually, there isn't such a thing. The term is an oxymoron—it contradicts itself. Consider other oxymorons: thunderous silence; cruel kindness; sweet sorrow; airline food.

Just as nonsensical is the expression "spirit-filled grouch" or "gloomy Christian." It is a contradiction of terms. By definition, a Christian is one in whom Christ lives. And where Christ is, there is joy. In the words of Joseph Marmion, "Joy is the echo of God's life within us."

This joy is available regardless of circumstances. Often people think joy comes with things. Or with talent. Or with marriage.

Take, for example, the miserable 36-year-old woman who desperately wanted a husband. Every night she hung a pair of men's pants on her bed and prayed:

> Father in heaven, hear my prayer,
> And grant it if You can;
> I've hung a pair of trousers here,
> Please fill them with a man!

Perhaps you've been guilty of thinking, I'd be happy . . . if I could get married . . . if I could buy a new Porsche . . . if I were a rap star . . . if I were as good-looking as . . .

The happiest people are rarely the richest or the most beautiful. They do not find joy in the externals. Rather, they enjoy what they have and don't get suckered into believing the absurd notion that having more money, or more brains, or more of anything, will make them happy.

Joyful people understand the internal reality of Christ living within. Consequently, we can describe them with the redundant phrase "joyful Christian."

POSITIVE ATTITUDE

LEAKING POISON

Are you a complainer? If you made a record of a typical day's conversations, would it look something like this?

6:45 a.m.	"Ugggghhhhhhh! I hate mornings."
7:00 a.m.	"Mom, she's taking too long in the shower."
7:15 a.m.	"Do we have to have oatmeal *again*?"
7:45 a.m.	"Get out of my seat, you punk."
8:15 a.m.	"I wish I was a jock like Greg Jenkins."
8:30 a.m.	"She's my least favorite of all the substitute teachers."
9:00 a.m.	"Hurry up, recess; she's as boring as a bear in January."
9:30 a.m.	"I always get stuck in right field."
10:00 a.m.	"A surprise quiz? That's not fair."
11:00 a.m.	"The way Jesse stares at her all the time is disgusting."
12:00 noon	"See if I eat lunch with her again. She's such a porker she puts mayonnaise on her Tylenol."
1:00 p.m.	"Why's the teacher always picking on me?"
2:00 p.m.	"You know what I heard about Marty?"
3:00 p.m.	"You call this a car?"
4:00 p.m.	"Mom! How come you opened my mail?"
5:00 p.m.	"Someone's been snooping in my room again."

6:00 p.m.	"Do I have to go to prayer meeting?"
6:01 p.m.	"I don't have anything to wear."
7:00 p.m.	"Pastor Montgomery is a talking Sominex."
8:00 p.m.	"Dad, I wanted to stay and talk to Leslie."
9:00 p.m.	"How do you expect me to do my homework without the stereo turned on?"
10:00 p.m.	"What do you think I am? A little kid? It's only 10:00."

Without realizing it, complaining can become a way of life. Of course, the people around the complainer notice the subtle, leaking poison, but the complainer drools toxins and often fails to notice the lethal results. But every complaining word damages our friendships.

Can you imagine how much fun it would be to chum around with a person who never complains or gossips or whines? Why not be that kind of friend today?

"DO EVERYTHING WITHOUT COMPLAINING" (PHIL. 2:14).

CONTENTMENT

DUMB AS A FOX

A fox had discovered a vineyard—but a fence surrounded the vineyard on all sides. Although the fox found a hole in the fence, it was too narrow. So the fox fasted for three days until he became quite slim, and thus he managed to get through the hole.

Then he ate the grapes. But in doing so, he again became fat.

When the fox was ready to leave the vineyard again, he couldn't get through the hole. After fasting for another three days to become slim, he managed to escape.

Once outside, he glanced at the vineyard and said,

"Vineyard, you and your fruits are good! Everything within you is beautiful and praiseworthy But of what use are you? The way one enters you is also the way in which one leaves you."

And so it is with the world.*

"BUT GODLINESS WITH CONTENTMENT IS GREAT GAIN. FOR WE BROUGHT NOTHING INTO THE WORLD, AND WE CAN TAKE NOTHING OUT OF IT" (1 TIM. 6:6, 7).

* "The Fox and the Vineyard" from *Our Masters Taught: Rabbinic Stories and Sayings*, by Jacob J. Petuchowski. © 1982. Reprinted by permission of The Crossroad Publishing Company, New York.

THREE COMMANDMENTS OF CONTENTMENT

If you could trade lives with Julia Roberts, would you? How about exchanging with Bill Clinton? Or Michael Jordan? Or are you content with who you are and what you have?

Being satisfied is an essential ingredient of success. Consider the three commandments of contentment.

I. Thou shalt live in the present.

> I was regretting the past
> And fearing the future . . .
> Suddenly my Lord was speaking:
> "My name is I AM." He paused.
> I waited. He continued,
>
> "When you live in the past,
> with its mistakes and regrets,
> it is hard. I am not there.
> My name is not I WAS.

"When you live in the future,
with its problems and fears,
it is hard. I am not there.
My name is not I WILL BE.

"When you live in this moment,
it is not hard.
I am here.
My name is I AM."*

Avoid the traps of wishing, hoping, and regretting. Invest in the now. Be satisfied with yourself today.

II. Thou shalt be thankful.

Rudyard Kipling was a highly successful author in his lifetime, but a British newspaper constantly printed critical comments about him. It reported, "He just writes for the money. One word of Rudyard Kipling today is worth $100."

Shortly after the unkind article appeared, a reporter cornered Kipling and said, "So you're worth $100 a word, are you? Here's a $100 bill. Now write me one word." With this he handed him a paper and pencil.

Kipling took the $100, put it in his pocket, and on the paper wrote one word: "Thanks!"

Today, increase the number of times you say thank you. See if you don't feel more content.

III. Thou shalt not whine.

Life is unfair and pain inevitable, but misery is optional. So when life dumps on you, don't whine. Rather, be content through the ditches of life. Apply the advice of Ann Landers:

"If I were asked to give what I consider the single most useful bit of advice for all humanity, it would be this: Expect trouble as an inevitable part of life, and when it comes, hold your head high, look it squarely in the eye, and say, "I will be bigger than you. You cannot defeat me."

---

*"I Am" by Helen Mallicoat, originally published in *Holy Sweat*, Tim Hansel, 1987, Word Publishing, Dallas, Texas. All rights reserved.

Consider the company T-shirt I saw that software giant, Microsoft, manufactured: "When danger comes, we stare it in the face and laugh our heads off."

HAPPINESS

HAPPINESS ISN'T...

Two teardrops were floating down the river of life. The second teardrop asked the first, "Who are you?"

The first replied, "I am a teardrop from a girl who loved a man and lost him. Who are you?"

The second responded, "I am a teardrop from the girl who got him."

Sometimes we cry over things we cannot have. But sometimes we would have cried more had we received them.

Isn't it ironic how our quest for happiness can end with the opposite result? The Lite beer commercials promise happiness but say nothing about puking at 1:00 a.m. The steamy TV shows don't mention herpes. The Lexus flyer doesn't advertise the enslaving payment book as thick as a Bible. Things that promise happiness may not deliver.

Popularity won't guarantee happiness. Nor will money. Not even beauty can deliver. Consider Brigitte Bardot, the sex symbol who enjoyed the accolades of fans for many years. Now approaching her 60s, she doesn't sound too happy:

"Bardot . . . lives with . . . several dogs, cats, and a donkey. 'I have not bought a dress in 10 years . . . I don't polish my nails, and I go to the hairdresser perhaps once a year. . . . I have to accept old age, right? It is horrible; you rot; you fall to pieces; you stink. It scares me more than anything else. . . . There's a beach not far away, but I never go there during the day. . . . I'm not so pretty. I wouldn't inflict this sight on anyone anymore.'"*

Beauty fades. Fame can't guarantee happiness. Popularity alone won't bring happiness.

In the end happiness cannot come from the outside, but only from the inside. Success is learning to be happy without externals like cars, good looks, and applause. As Storm Jameson says: "Happiness comes of the capacity to feel deeply, to enjoy simply, to think freely, to be needed."

"TO THE MAN WHO PLEASES HIM, GOD GIVES . . . HAPPINESS,
BUT TO THE SINNER HE GIVES THE TASK OF GATHERING AND
STORING UP WEALTH TO HAND IT OVER TO THE ONE
WHO PLEASES GOD" (ECCL. 2:26).

---

*From the book, *Graduating Into Happiness* by Joe McGloin. Copyright © 1988 by Baker Book House Company. Used by permission.

Depression

Five Surefire Ways to Brighten Your Days

Presenting: the blue day. Starring: me. Time: last Monday. Weather: cold and cloudy. The story: Last Monday, in an absolute frenzy, I was racing to the supermarket and failed to see an elderly woman at the crosswalk. I missed her by a city block and missed squashing her poodle by at least three hairs. The officer thought it was more like one hair.

Undaunted, I marched into Piggly Wiggly to buy two loaves of bread and one pack of Charmin. The Cracker Jacks stand was strategically positioned in my way. I brushed one box. One box!

Are you familiar with the domino theory? The collapse of the leaning tower of Cracker Jacks caused everyone in the store to stare.

"Oh, hi!" beamed one shopper I hardly recognized. "Haven't seen you for a while."

"Oh, hi!" I quipped through a strained smile.

"You look great! A few less hairs than when we played ball at the Y, but you look good."

Yes it was quite the day. The kind of day that makes even the most well-balanced, self-assured person feel blue. How did I feel? Clumsy, bald, and blue—not just blue, deep navy blue.

But then who hasn't felt that way? We all have days when every silver lining has a cloud. The "blues"—or depression—is considered to be the most common form of mental illness in the United States. The National Institute of Mental Health estimates 200 million people suffer from this problem each year. At any given moment, up to 5 percent of the population in the United States is depressed. Twice as many women report the illness as men. And the incidence of depression has been rising—especially among teens and young adults.

So next time you lose your contact lens, your boyfriend, and your job in the same afternoon, take heart. If the "black dog," as Winston Churchill called his depression, starts biting you, don't ignore it. Take this over-the-counter prescription to beat the blues:

1. Soak up the joy of kids. Go to the hospital maternity ward or the playground or a day-care center and watch kids.

2. Go nuts! Do something ridiculous with your best friend and laugh yourselves silly. Spend a half hour trying on eccentric clothes you would never wear. Cram into a photo booth at the mall. Try on Tina Turner wigs.

3. Do a random act of senseless kindness. Buy a dozen doughnuts and give one to the cashier as you leave. Pay for the car behind you at a toll booth. Write a long letter to your grandma. Deliver a hamburger to your favorite puppy at the pet shop. Compliment three people today.

4. Call someone who is more miserable than you are. Best bets include anyone who just got dumped or fired. Let your friend do all the talking.

5. Get lots of sunshine and exercise. Jog, throw snowballs, play volleyball. Anything that is fun and vigorous will do.

"YOU HAVE MADE KNOWN TO ME THE PATH OF LIFE; YOU WILL FILL ME WITH JOY IN YOUR PRESENCE" (PS. 16:11).

SELF-ESTEEM

EVER FEEL WORTHLESS?

Do you ever feel stupid or awkward or worthless? Don't sweat it too hard. Even superstars question their value and purpose in life.

Here's an exercise. Match the quote of self-doubt with the superstar who said it.

Superstars

A. Marilyn Monroe

B. Joe Theismann

C. Dolly Parton

D. Dustin Hoffman

E. Larry Bird

F. Richard Nixon

G. Jane Fonda

H. Gary Cooper

I. Michael Jordon

J. John McEnroe

K. Kevin Costner

L. Muhammad Ali

Quotations

1. _____ "The general consensus seems to be that I don't act at all."
2. _____ "Life stinks."
3. _____ "I hate fighting."
4. _____ "I hope there's no one else like me."
5. _____ "Scrubbing floors and emptying bedpans has as much dignity as the presidency."
6. _____ "I wish I came in first more often."
7. _____ "Can you imagine anybody wanting to look this way for real?"
8. _____ "Being a celebrity is like rape."
9. _____ "I wish I were smart, more disciplined, and better read."
10. _____ "No one ever called me pretty when I was a little girl."
11. _____ "I was never one of the boys."
12. _____ "Just because I have a few more dollars in my pocket doesn't mean I'm better than somebody else."

WHAT? God designed you for a unique purpose. "We are God's workmanship, created in Christ Jesus to do good works, which God prepared in advance for us to do" (Eph. 2:10).

SO WHAT? I'm weird. I like to watch a video until it's over—I mean *over* over. While some race to the bathroom, others start returning the empty popcorn bowls to the kitchen, and someone starts folding the blankets, I sit. And stare.

44

For many, the movie is over when the couple kiss and walk into the sunset. For me, the movie isn't over until I've read all the credits: the "secretary" whose only line was a shriek when "robber 3" grabbed her purse.

By reading the credits, I make a subtle statement: everyone is important. Not just the superstars (who doubt themselves and question their worth too), but the no-names who make up the background. They matter.

That's the message Christ proclaimed. He gave star status to no-names. He created every one of us for a unique purpose. You matter to God.

NOW WHAT? Why not make an effort today to show that every person matters to God?

- Write a few notes to friends affirming their worth.
- Look for opportunities to tell people they are making a difference.
- Explore the question What unique purpose has God called me to fulfill?

Answer key: 1. H. 2. D. 3. L. 4. G. 5. F. 6. I. 7. C. 8. J. 9. K. 10. A. 11. B. 12. E.

SELF-CONFIDENCE

HERE LIES PAUL NEWMAN

Other kids collected stamps and coins and baseball cards and buttons and postcards and . . . Not me. As a kid my hobby was autographed pictures. I still have treasured albums full of fading photos of famous people: Gerald Ford, Evel Knievel, Farrah Fawcett, Hank Aaron, Cher, John Denver, etc.

And I still get twitterpated when I see someone famous. Recently in a restaurant I sat near K. C. Jones, the former basketball great. It was all my wife could do to keep me from slurping the corn chowder he dripped by his Nikes. Another time I saw Richard Nixon. And more recently I passed Bob Hope on the sidewalk. I am still awed around celebrities.

Not too long ago I read a true story that made me laugh because it sounded like something that could have happened to me:

"A tourist was standing in line to buy an ice-cream cone at a Thrifty Drug store in Beverly Hills. To her utter shock and amazement, who should walk in and stand right behind her but Paul Newman! Well, the lady, even though she was rattled, determined to maintain her composure. She purchased her ice-cream cone and turned confidently and exited the store.

"However, to her horror, she realized that she had left the counter without her ice-cream cone! She waited a few minutes till she felt all was clear, and then went back into the store to claim her cone. As she approached the counter, the cone was not in the little circular receptacle, and for a moment she stood there pondering what might have happened to it. Then feeling a polite tap on her shoulder, she turned and was confronted by—you guessed it—Paul Newman. The famous actor then told the lady that if she was looking for her ice-cream cone, she had put it into her purse!"

And yet even Paul Newman sometimes questions his value: "I look like I'm having fun, but I should be having more fun than I'm having. In work I'm not happy because it will never be good enough. My epitaph might read 'Here lies Paul Newman who died a flop because his eyes turned brown.' "*

Hollywood paints portraits of fantasy, and we lap it up. If we could see our idols as they see themselves, it would jolt us into their reality of self-doubt.

But if we could see ourselves as God views us, it would knock us into the reality of self-confidence. For God designed you unlike anybody else. You are uniquely valuable. Anything valuable that you will contribute to the world will come through the expression of your own identity, that single spark of divinity that sets you apart from every other living creature.

---

*Robert Scheer, "The Further Adventures of Paul Newman," *Esquire*, Oct. 1989, p. 168.

"EACH ONE SHOULD TEST HIS OWN ACTIONS. THEN HE CAN
TAKE PRIDE IN HIMSELF, WITHOUT COMPARING HIMSELF
TO SOMEBODY ELSE" (GAL. 6:4).

WHAT MICHELLE PFEIFFER NEEDS IS . . .

Actress Michelle Pfeiffer's picture appeared on the cover of a magazine with the caption "What Michelle Pfeiffer Needs Is . . . Absolutely Nothing!"

To need nothing! Wouldn't that be nice? If I didn't have a bald head? and pimples? and a big nose?

An astute reporter later discovered, however, that Michelle Pfeiffer did need something after all.

Michelle Pfeiffer? Needs something? No!

She needed more than $1,500 worth of touch-up work on that cover photo. Quoting the touch-up artist's bill, here is a partial list of things that were done to make Michelle Pfeiffer appear perfect:

"Clean up complexion, soften eye lines, soften smile line, add color to lips, trim chin, remove neck lines, soften line under earlobe, add highlights to earrings, add blush to cheek, clean up neckline, remove stray hair, remove hair strands on dress, adjust color and add hair on top of head [*Hey! I like that idea!*], add dress on side to create better line, add to forehead, add dress on shoulder, soften neck muscle a bit, clean up and smooth dress folds under arm, and create one seam on image on right side."

Total price: $1,525.*

God, I watch TV and fantasize about having it all together like

*Reprinted from *Hot Illustrations for Youth Talks,* copyright 1994 by Youth Specialities, Inc., 1224 Greenfield Dr., El Cajon, CA 92021. Used by permission.

Seinfeld or Meg Ryan or Hakeem Olajuwon or Michelle Pfeiffer.

Remind me it's plastic. Remind me that Hollywood creates an image that is bogus. Remind me that the stars have needs just like me.

Give me the courage to swim against the current of Hollywood and strive for internal beauty rather than external facades.

"YOUR BEAUTY SHOULD NOT COME FROM OUTWARD ADORNMENT, SUCH AS BRAIDED HAIR AND THE WEARING OF GOLD JEWELRY AND FINE CLOTHES. INSTEAD, IT SHOULD BE THAT OF YOUR INNER SELF, THE UNFADING BEAUTY OF A GENTLE AND QUIET SPIRIT, WHICH IS OF GREAT WORTH IN GOD'S SIGHT" (1 PETER 3:3, 4).

SELF-ACCEPTANCE

THE INGREDIENTS FOR LIKING YOURSELF

A zillion "experts" today claim to have discovered the secret ingredient for feeling better about ourselves. Suggestions include: Blow yourself a kiss in the mirror every day. Wear a button that says "I am lovable and capable." Change your hairstyle. Get better grades. Repeat "I am special" 762 times a day. Get your nose pierced. Whisper warm fuzzies to your inner self. The list goes on and on and on and . . .

Liking yourself isn't something you can buy. Other people can't make you happy about and able to appreciate yourself. That deep-down-inside-the-skin feeling that you are worth a lot comes only by cultivating inner qualities. Once you understand this, you can develop these ingredients to like yourself.

1. Kindness. Too few people have discovered this ingredient for liking ourselves. Jay Leno tells of how he once chided a supermarket clerk for failing to say thank you, only for her to snap back, "It's printed on your receipt!" My guess is the clerk doesn't like herself much.

Everyone can express kindness. Kindness means you smile. Kindness prompts you to sit next to the new redhead from Arkansas when you'd rather eat lunch with "the gang." Kindness means you listen to your aunt Maggie tell the same story for the trillionth time. Kindness helps you chuckle at your dad's stale joke for the tillyzeptrillionth time. It's keeping a secret, passing on a compliment, honoring your word.

The better we treat others, the more we like ourselves. Look for ways to show kindness and notice how you feel about yourself.

2. Integrity. Four high school boys afflicted with spring fever skipped morning classes. After lunch they reported to the teacher that their car had had a flat tire. Much to their relief, she smiled and said, "Well, you missed a test this morning, so take seats apart from one another and get out your notebooks."

Still smiling, she waited for them to settle down. Then she said, "First question: Which tire was flat?"

Dishonesty always comes back to sting us. Even if no one discovers the truth, you like yourself less when you compromise what is right. You can read every book on self-esteem, but if you are dishonest, you have no right to feel good about yourself. And I promise, you won't. Integrity is the cornerstone of liking yourself.

It's not what we do or who we know that makes us like ourselves. Rather, it's what we are. Feeling good about yourself goes deeper than just doing—it comes from being.

3. Productivity. One of the seven deadly sins in the Middle Ages was laziness. It's pretty hard to feel good about yourself when your biggest accomplishment for the week was guzzling a six-pack of Squirt and devouring a bag of Cheetos. But it's pretty hard not to feel good about yourself when you look at the acre of lawn you mowed or you finish the last sentence of a term paper. Being productive builds self-esteem.

"TO THOSE WHO BY PERSISTENCE IN DOING GOOD SEEK GLORY,

HONOR AND IMMORTALITY, HE WILL GIVE ETERNAL LIFE. BUT
FOR THOSE WHO ARE SELF-SEEKING AND WHO REJECT THE
TRUTH AND FOLLOW EVIL, THERE WILL BE WRATH
AND ANGER" (ROM. 2:7, 8).

GUILT

FIVE WAYS TO HANDLE GUILT

Have you ever felt guilty? We all have. So here are five suggestions on how to handle guilt:

1. Determine if your guilt is valid. Mr. Barwick had a cir-
culation problem in his leg but refused to allow the recom-
mended amputation. As the pain became unbearable, though, he
finally consented to the surgeon's advice.

Before the operation, however, he asked the doctor, "What do
you do with legs after they are removed?"

"We do a biopsy, then we incinerate them," the doctor
replied. "Why do you ask?"

Mr. Barwick made a bizarre request: "I would like you to pre-
serve my leg in a pickling jar. I will put it on my mantle. Then I
can taunt it and get even for the pain it has caused me."

He got his wish. But the despised leg had the last laugh.

Mr. Barwick suffered from the condition known as phantom
limb. Somewhere locked in the brains of amputees a memory
lingers of the nonexistent hand or leg. Invisible toes curl, imaginary hands grasp things, an amputated leg feels sturdy enough
to stand on. Despite the fact that the amputated leg rested on his
mantle, Mr. Barwick could still feel the torturous pressure of the
swelling as the muscles cramped.

So it is with false guilt. The taunting pain whispers of shame
that is nonexistent. False guilt is common: guilt about your par-

ents' divorce, guilt over abuse in your childhood, guilt about your failure to live up to your parents' ideals. False guilt clings like a sticky spider's web.

However, we need to take care of true guilt. It is like a flashing light on the dashboard showing the engine doesn't have enough oil. You can take care of the flashing light by smashing it with a hammer. Or you can address the real problem and add oil. True guilt is the warning light that alerts you to something deeper that is wrong.

2. Be specific. Determine why you feel guilty. Here is the difference between true and false guilt. True guilt is usually about something specific. Once you have isolated the actual reason you feel guilty, you can go to step 3.

3. Confess your sin. Have you ever had a super-sensitive, under-the-skin pimple that grows to the size of a grape before you can pop it? It's painful when it finally bursts, but that is when healing begins.

So it is with sin. It festers under the skin, growing more and more uncomfortable, until you confess it. Although it may be painful, it is only at that point of confession that healing can actually start.

4. Accept God's forgiveness. A priest in the Philippines, a much-loved man of God, felt guilty about a secret sin he had committed many years before. He asked God again and again to forgive him, but he still felt guilty.

In his church was a woman who deeply loved God and claimed she talked to Him and He talked to her. The priest, however, didn't believe it. To test her he said, "The next time you talk to God, I want you to ask Him what sin your priest committed while he was in the seminary." The woman agreed.

A few days later the priest asked, "Well, did you talk with God lately?"

"Yes, I have," she replied.

"And did you ask Him what sin I committed?"

"Yes, I did."

"Well, what did He say?"

"He said, 'I don't remember.'"

If you ask God to forgive you, He does! Accept His forgiveness and move on.

5. Expect the natural consequences. Even though we confess and receive forgiveness, sin still has consequences. Students who cheat in algebra—although they can be forgiven—may never enjoy the teacher's trust as they once did. Teenagers who sleep around—although they can be saved—may suffer with herpes. Sin has natural consequences, but it can always be buried in God's grace.

"LET US DRAW NEAR TO GOD WITH A SINCERE HEART IN FULL ASSURANCE OF FAITH, HAVING OUR HEARTS SPRINKLED TO CLEANSE US FROM A GUILTY CONSCIENCE AND HAVING OUR BODIES WASHED WITH PURE WATER" (HEB. 10:22).

STRESS

HOW TO WIN THE RAT RACE

Biology test tomorrow. The soccer game after school. Mom's nagging you to clean the garage. Algebra assignment is due at 4:00. Dad's badgering you to mow the lawn. Your girlfriend wants you to call her. You need to write to Uncle Hank. You promised to teach the youth group lesson this week in church.

Does the rat race ever stop? No! But consider these suggestions from Solomon on how to handle the pressure:

1. Line up your priorities. I am prepared to die. I have been since I wrote my will. While many Americans have written their plans for after death, less than 2 percent have put down their plans for life. Wouldn't it make more sense to write out goals for living rather than dying? The trip is easier if you know where you are going.

One of the reasons life gets so harried is that we fail to determine what is most important. The first step to winning the rat race is to list your priorities. Solomon tells us the fool lives a scattered life, racing here and there and everywhere, but the wise person stays focused on what is important. "A discerning man keeps wisdom in view, but a fool's eyes wander to the ends of the earth" (Prov. 17:24).

2. Lighten up your attitude. To paraphrase Solomon: Chill out! Remember the two rules of life. First rule: Don't sweat the small stuff. Second rule: It's all small stuff.

Consider the following information from *USA Today:*

"When stress hits, having a good cry is apt to make it worse, but humor helps ward off anxiety and depression, a new study shows. Weeping may backfire because it convinces people they must be in bad shape. . . . [Susan] Labott and fellow psychologist Randall Martin of Northern Illinois University at DeKalb surveyed 714 men and women. Key findings:

"1. At comparable stress levels, criers were more depressed, anxious, hostile, and tired than those who wept less.

"2. Those who use humor the most are most successful at combating stress. 'These are the kind of people who try to find something funny about their predicament,' Labott says. 'Or in a tense situation, they look for something funny to say.'"*

A child laughs an average of 400 times a day. Compare that to the average adult at 15 laughs a day, and you begin to understand why all the stress!

"A cheerful heart is good medicine, but a crushed spirit dries up the bones" (Prov. 17:22).

3. Look up to God. As you focus on God, your perspective changes. It's like soaking in the panoramic view from a mountaintop. You see things in a broader perspective.

I love the story of the boy playing baseball by himself. As he strutted through the backyard he mused to himself, "I'm the greatest baseball player in the world!" Tossing the ball into the air, he took a Babe Ruth swing and missed. Undaunted, he said, "I'm the greatest baseball player in the world." Again he threw the ball and swung, only to miss again. "Wow!" he exclaimed. "What a pitcher!"

It's all in how you look at it. Look up to God, and your per-

---

*Marilyn Elias, "Laughter May Help More Than a Good Cry," *USA Today,* June 17, 1987, p. 1.

spective will broaden.

"TRUST IN THE LORD WITH ALL YOUR HEART AND LEAN NOT ON YOUR OWN UNDERSTANDING; IN ALL YOUR WAYS ACKNOWLEDGE HIM, AND HE WILL MAKE YOUR PATHS STRAIGHT" (PROV. 3:5, 6).

WORRY

WORRY WARS

It ain't no use putting up your umbrella till it rains," my grandpa would say. Sounds good, but who can escape the battle of worry?

Jesus shared some insights in Matthew 6:25-34 about the worry wars. He said, "Don't worry, be happy" (KHT—Karl Haffner Translation). Then He gave three steps about how to stop worrying.

1. Trust God. Jesus concedes that wicked people should worry but asks why Christians do. After all, they have God to take care of them. As Mahatma Gandhi said: "There is nothing that wastes the body like worry, and one who has any faith in God should be ashamed to worry about anything whatsoever."

Jesus said: "So do not worry, saying, 'What shall we eat?' or 'What shall we drink?' or 'What shall we wear?' For the pagans run after all these things, and your heavenly Father knows that you need them" (Matt. 6:31, 32).

2. Seek God first. Recently I read of a car accident in Salem, Oregon, that killed three college students. Authorities said the collision occurred when the driver swerved to miss a dead cat.

Three lives. To miss a dead cat. How tragic.

Tragic too are lives that swerve out of control reacting to petty obstacles. Don't worry about dead cats. Rather, focus on the important things, like knowing God. "But seek first [God's] kingdom and his righteousness, and all these things will be given to you as well" (verse 33).

3. Live one day at a time. Most students agreed that Mrs. Kirback was a pit bull. Just thinking about her class made even my fingernails sweat. I was so worried about it that I studied the textbook all summer to prepare. I stuck to *Wilson's Illustrated World History Book* like bubble gum to Reeboks—only to discover the following year that Mrs. Kirback had changed the textbook for the class!

As it turned out, it didn't matter. Mrs. Kirback proved to be quite human. My months of worry had been totally useless. I did, however, learn one valuable lesson from her: wait until class starts to study—in case the teacher changes the textbook!

> "THEREFORE DO NOT WORRY ABOUT TOMORROW, FOR TOMORROW WILL WORRY ABOUT ITSELF" (MATT. 6:34).

BITTERNESS

SATAN'S GARAGE SALE

Satan had a garage sale. Did you hear about it? His tools were on sale to anyone willing to pay the price. Pride, envy, lust, anger, and deceit were but a few of the classics on display.

In the corner was a wedge-shaped tool. Scrapes and scratches marked its handle. The iron head was worn and dull. The tattered canvas case disclosed a lifetime of use. In spite of its condition, however, the tool displayed a price tag higher than any other.

"Why in this hell," a curious shopper asked, "would that old tool be so expensive?"

"Ahhhhh," the devil smirked. "That's my most useful tool. I call it bitterness. With it I can dig into a teenager's heart and live forever. I love my tool of bitterness."

Bitterness destroys. Left unchecked, it festers like a cancer. It taints our friendships, our feelings, and our future. Even justified bitterness ruins our lives.

The girl abused by her stepfather has a right to feel bitter. The boy raised by a mother screaming "You'll never amount to anything!" is justified in his angry feelings. Nonetheless, this bitterness destroys not the abuser, but the abused.

Healing such bitterness may take years. Confronting it may cause pain. But ignoring it will be worse.

Healing begins when we face the cause head-on. The journey toward wholeness begins when we step into the canyon of hurt and explore why the festering wound is inside us. As we examine it, our discoveries help us. We begin to like others more. We like God more. And we begin to love ourselves.

"GET RID OF ALL BITTERNESS. . . . BE KIND AND COMPASSIONATE
TO ONE ANOTHER, FORGIVING EACH OTHER, JUST AS IN CHRIST
GOD FORGAVE YOU" (EPH. 4:31, 32).

SHAME

THE GIRL WHO DIED TWICE

Rebecca Thompson fell twice from the Fremont Canyon Bridge. She died both times. The first time she shattered her spirit. The second time she broke her neck.

It happened in Casper, Wyoming. She was only 18 when a pair of thugs bullied her and her 11-year-old sister into a car and drove 40 miles southwest to the Fremont Canyon Bridge.

On that bridge the hoodlums raped and beat Rebecca, then threw both girls over the ledge into the river 112 feet below. Her sister died upon impact with the rocks below.

Rebecca survived. Sort of.

She ricocheted into deeper water and sustained deep cuts, ugly gashes, and a hip fractured in five places.

She lived. Kind of.

Doctors mended her wounds and brought healing to her hip. Prosecutors brought her attackers to justice. Friends attempted to help Rebecca process the pain.

As I said, she lived. But not really.

The horror of that canyon still lingered. And in September 1992, 19 years later, she returned to that bridge.

Again she was not alone. This time she came with her boyfriend and their 2-year-old daughter. Together they sat on the ledge of the Fremont Canyon Bridge. Tears spilled toward the river below as Rebecca relived the searing memory. Not wanting the child to see her mom in such pain, the boyfriend carried the toddler to the car.

And that's when he heard her body hit the water.

Rebecca died. Again. Her journey into her canyon of shame had come to its sad end.

Maybe you too have a canyon of shame. Maybe you know the ache of being violated. Raped. Abused. Molested. Shamed.

Maybe you keep trying to outrun the tentacles of yesterday's shame—but they stretch further than your hope. They drag you back into that canyon. And you wonder, *Will I ever escape?*

Jesus came to answer that question. For you—along with all the other Rebecca Thompsons in the world—Jesus walks into the canyon. Not to condemn, but to comfort. Not to hammer, but to heal. Not to destroy, but to defend.

He comes to lead you out of the canyon. For the canyon is too rugged to escape alone. You need help. You don't have to die there as Rebecca Thompson did.

Won't you take His hand and begin that long journey upward? Invite Christ to the Fremont Bridge of your world. Let Him stand with you in your canyon.

Grip His hand tightly. Feel His blood drip. Squeeze His hand and let His blood heal your soul.

Be reminded that He knows what being a victim is about. He feels the pain of being used and understands shame.

And marvel at His strength. His understanding. His compassion. But mostly, marvel at His grace.

"FOR GOD DID NOT SEND HIS SON INTO THE WORLD TO
CONDEMN THE WORLD, BUT TO SAVE THE WORLD
THROUGH HIM" (JOHN 3:17).

Succeeding in Relationships

3

Communication

The Secret to Bruise-free Living

You parasail ever?" the man asked in broken English.

"No," I replied as he strapped me into a contraption that looked like a full body diaper. "But it doesn't look too hard."

"When boat goes, you . . ." The Mexican rambled on in a language I barely understood. My mind drifted as I gazed at the white beaches of Acapulco.

"Now, senor, red flag vairdy, vairdy important means . . ."

I flinched a bit as he tightened the strap against my sunburn.

"And dis white flag when I wave is . . ."

Breathing deeply, I savored the salty aroma.

"Dat's it!" the Mexican screamed to the boat driver as I was whisked off my feet.

Faster than I could say "Adios, amigos," I was floating 300 feet above the water. "Woooooweeeee!" I screamed. I was having more fun than a flea at a dog show. Until the landing.

As the boat circled around, I descended toward the guy who was frantically waving his red flag. I strained to remember what he had said about that flag. Although I could vaguely recall him saying it was "vairdy important," I couldn't remember what it meant.

Suddenly I found myself plummeting toward a beach hut with the speed of a scud missile. Tourists below scurried out of the way as if a small asteroid were about to blast a crater on the beach. The man with the flag screamed expletives at me that my publisher won't print.

I kept drifting right ("starboard") toward the beach hut (Dagaberto's Delicious Drinks) until I crashed into it with the force of a refrigerator (William Perry), smashing margaritas that instantly belonged to me ($67.83). Fortunately, besides a scolding ("You never parasail here again, you #&*#*!"), all I got was a bruise larger than my skin surface area.

Oh, yeah—I also got a lesson in communication.

Had I listened, I would have known that the red flag meant to pull on the ropes to activate the parachute's brakes. But somewhere in the communication process that tidbit got lost.

Of course, no one claims that communication is easy, and yet it's difficult to survive without it. Communication is the key that opens three doors to understanding.

Understanding People

Understanding is the first step in appreciating anything. Maybe you'll never fully grasp everything about your siblings or your parents or your teacher, but if you want to be successful in your relationships, you *must* communicate with them. Straightforward communication opens doors to understanding people.

Understanding Life

Through communication we discover answers to life's probing questions, such as: What does "cowabunga" mean? Why do onions make people cry? Why is it that we drive on a parkway and park in a driveway?

By communicating the right questions, we discover answers: "Cowabunga" is from 1960s Australia and is a surfer's exclamation of delight. And it's the volatile oil in onions that contains sulfuric acid that makes us cry. As for parking in a driveway, I'm still asking.

Understanding God

Only by reading, and talking, and listening to God do we understand Him. As we walk with Him, and laugh, and share, and ask questions, and vent our anger, we discover—almost unnoticeably—that in this process of communicating we have a new Friend.

Communication is the key to opening doors of understanding. It can also be the key to saving your body (and the surroundings) from bruises.

Parents

Living in Your Arranged Marriage

You come home from school and plop yourself on the sofa to faze out with reruns of *Gilligan's Island*. Then your thoughts drift to fonder images of your close encounter with "Blue Eyes" in geometry class.

Suddenly your mom interrupts your fantasy. "I think we met the perfect match for you today—Leslie. Yes! We've decided it's Leslie for you."

Not that your opinion matters, but you saw Leslie once at a youth rally in Pocatello, Idaho, and your heart didn't flutter. Not that Leslie's ugly, but freckles and braces aren't your thing. Also, you would prefer someone at least as tall as you.

But your parents have been scouring the social circles for years, and they're convinced Leslie is the one. So after the formal introductions you and Leslie get married and move in together, even though you are strangers.

Does it seem too ludicrous? It's not unlike a number of situations in which you already find yourself.

Think about it. You had no choice in who your parents would be. Did you choose your brother or sister? Chances are you didn't pick your teacher. Yet you are forced to live with these people, whom you did not select. The results can be as disastrous as an arranged marriage—but not necessarily.

Even today a large number of the marriages in the world are arranged. Many such relationships are strong and fulfilling. Likewise, your own everyday "arranged marriages" can also work.

It's not easy. Chances are your parents and siblings and teachers occasionally misunderstand you. They too have junk they're trying to make sense of. Nevertheless, God asks you to accept them, freckles and all. Show them love, and God promises you will be happier and live longer.

"CHILDREN, OBEY YOUR PARENTS; THIS IS THE RIGHT THING TO DO BECAUSE GOD HAS PLACED THEM IN AUTHORITY OVER YOU. .... IF YOU HONOR YOUR FATHER AND MOTHER, YOURS WILL BE A LONG LIFE, FULL OF BLESSING" (EPH. 6:1-3, TLB).

DADS ARE FUNNY!

Dads are funny. I love my father, but he is funny. All dads are funny. They do strange and hilarious things—have you noticed?

Dads talk in funny ways. Have you observed how many times your dad will say something that doesn't make sense? For example, I heard a father say, "Young man, you look at me when I'm talking to you," followed instantly by "Don't you look at me like that." Some dads say, "If you cut off your legs playing around the lawn mower, don't come running to me!" Or my personal favorite: "Go get me something to hit you with." I'd fetch a balloon for the spanking: flabadubadub.

Dads sleep in funny ways. Have you ever discovered that Dad can sleep in any position at any time on the sofa? He's like a dead walrus—until you touch the remote control. Suddenly he bellows, "Hey, I was watching the second round of the Dinah Shore Golf Classic." Let him watch his show, and he drifts back to sleep with a contented smile.

Dads act in funny ways. They have strange habits. My dad will never take a second piece of pie and just eat it. Instead, he will cut it in half and eat it. Then he'll dissect the half piece and on and on, until he's splitting slivers of pie. He claims "it's more temperate" that way.

Another funny habit dads have is they don't watch TV—they zap it. "Use Preparation H—" *Zap!* "Because you care enough to send—" *Zap!* "Tastes great! Less filling!—" *Zap!* From Tootsie Rolls to Whoppers to Tidy Bowl to Scotch Tape, Dads channel-surf around the stations in the endless search for something to watch.

Like kids and moms and uncles—and everyone—dads are funny. In spite of their funny ways, however, we are to respect them. He is dad, which means God has given him authority and you should honor him. Who knows? There may be some dads who actually think teenagers are funny too.

"CHILDREN, OBEY YOUR PARENTS; THIS IS THE RIGHT THING TO
DO BECAUSE GOD HAS PLACED THEM IN AUTHORITY
OVER YOU" (EPH. 6:1, TLB).

MOMS ARE WEIRD!

While dads are funny, moms are weird! I like the Jewish proverb that states, "God could not be everywhere, and therefore He made mothers." Again, I love my mom, but she is weird.

Moms have weird imaginations. When God created your mom, He put a computer chip in her brain programmed to blow a circuit whenever you stay out too late. If you're a half hour late getting home, the computer kicks in. She knows what happened to you:

a. You were killed in a car wreck.

b. Your eccentric friends talked you into getting a full-body tattoo and now you're too sore to walk home.

c. You choked to death sucking on a Popsicle at Dairy Queen.

Your mom's weird imagination knows no bounds. Her computer has only one limit: it is not programmed to conclude that you might just have lost track of time.

Moms ask weird questions. Some of my personal favorites include: "What do you think I am? Stupid?" (How is a teenager supposed to answer that?) "What am I going to do with you?" (I don't know, Mom. What are your options?)

I suspect someday my mom will read this book and she'll ask me, "Do you really think I ask weird questions?"

Moms give weird answers. Ask any mom in the world why, and she'll reply with something such as: "Because I said so." Request one good reason, and she'll fire back: "Because I'm your mother." Or the scariest response from mom comes when you introduce her to your new heartthrob. Mom will inevitably respond with "So yoooooou're Stacey!"

When my mom reads this, I can't wait until she asks me why I wrote all this about moms. I've already got my answer: "Because I'm yooooooour son."

Moms are weird. But not to worry—we've all got our weird quirks. Enjoy your mom. She's weird only because she loves her kids and wants the best for them. For this, we should respect and obey her.

———

"IF YOU HONOR YOUR FATHER AND MOTHER, YOURS WILL BE A
LONG LIFE, FULL OF BLESSING" (EPH. 6:3, TLB).

SMOKING LITTLE TOES

My parents abused me. When I was 2 years old, I wanted to stick a fork in the electrical outlet and revel in the tingle. I longed to feel the rush of 110 volts coursing through my body. I aspired to suck on the end of that fork until my skin turned lavender and my little toes smoked. But my conservative, right-wing, traditional parents refused me that thrill. Can you believe it? They abused me!

As I grew older, the abuse continued. They refused me the exhilaration of playing kickball on Interstate 5. They would not let me drive until I got a permit. They denied me the excitement of drinking and drugs. My parents forbade many thrills that I desperately wanted to experience (at least at one point in my life).

Even though dads are funny and moms are weird, most parents have good motives. At times parents make mistakes, but usually their motives are right. This may not be much consolation if they just refused to let you go skiing this weekend, but sometimes it helps to know they act in love. Most parents don't stay up at night scheming how to make your life miserable. From their perspective, they simply want to keep you from sticking the fork in the electrical outlet.

As you grow older, the desire to stick a fork in the outlet begins to diminish (at least it should). Your needs and desires, however, don't go away. They change and become more complicated. At first your only concern was getting food in your belly when you were hungry. So your mom would feed you that repulsive green mashed stuff, and the hunger would go away. (Usually just looking at it would make the hunger go away.)

Now your desires are more complex. You need the Toyota this weekend for your date. You want to be accepted by your friends. You want good grades. You want a special friend. You need independence.

Trying to cope with these dynamics, parents naturally get confused about how to give you the freedom you need and yet protect you from getting burned by the outlet. It's difficult for parents. So try to put yourself in their shoes. (Even though they probably didn't have any at your age and had to walk 99 miles uphill both ways to school through the snow carrying three brothers and 10 sisters.)

"LISTEN TO YOUR FATHER AND MOTHER. WHAT YOU LEARN FROM THEM WILL STAND YOU IN GOOD STEAD; IT WILL GAIN YOU MANY HONORS" (PROV. 1:8, 9, TLB).

THE PERFECT SIZE

A nn Landers carried the story of a 9-year-old boy who went to town to buy his mother a birthday present. Browsing through J. C. Penny's lingerie department, he discovered a slip that seemed the perfect gift. The saleslady asked him what size his mother wore, and she wrapped it while he organized his nickels and dimes on the counter.

When the boy's mom opened the gift she squealed with delight—not mentioning that it was a size 8 rather than the ample size 22 that she really wore. "It's the most beautiful slip I've ever seen," she beamed. The child glowed with pride to see his mother so happy.

The next day the mother went to the store to exchange the slip. The saleslady remembered the woman's son vividly. She told the mother that when she had asked him what size his mother was, her son had replied, "She's just perfect."

Ann Landers added that she would withhold the name of the sender so moms everywhere could believe the letter came from their home.

Parents crave to feel honored by their kids—in spite of their flaws. Adults recognize their imperfections. Dad feels the sting of his temper. Mom knows the pain of her impatience. Your parents know they aren't the perfect size or the perfect Christians or the perfect disciplinarians. And yet they crave your love and respect.

Love sees beyond their imperfections. Love accepts. Love forgives. Love is not blind—it sees more, not less. Because it sees more, it is willing to see less.

"HONOR YOUR FATHER AND YOUR MOTHER, SO THAT YOU MAY LIVE LONG IN THE LAND THE LORD YOUR GOD IS GIVING YOU" (EX. 20:12).

Siblings

Seven Ways to Love Your Siblings

ighting among brothers and sisters has always been a problem. The first story about siblings in Scripture tells of Cain becoming so angry with his brother that he killed him. Before you get too excited with this option, remember that God was very angry at Cain.

The problem of warfare among brothers and sisters has been around for thousands of years, and one chapter of a book won't solve it. This chapter, however, can help you process and vent your feelings in a more productive way than bashing your brother's belly button. So before you give up and list your sister in the classifieds, try these seven tips on how to keep from pummeling your siblings.

1. Fight fair. The chance of brothers and sisters never squabbling is the same as Howard Stern becoming president. Fights are going to happen, but they don't have to make the national news—if you fight fair. Fighting fair means never physically or verbally attacking your brother or sister. Fight, but limit your conflict to the specific issue at hand.

2. Vent your anger in positive ways. Next time you get angry with your brother, before you reshape his head to look like a fortune cookie, give yourself some time to cool off and think of alternative ways of handling the dilemma. Find an outlet for your anger: take a walk, listen to your favorite CD, or bash on a tree stump with a baseball bat (your brother's belly button will thank you).

3. Set up rules to protect your privacy. The biggest cause of fights is the invasion of personal privacy. Set up "Don't you dare touch" zones in your closets and drawers. You need your space, and the same is true of your brothers and sisters. Don't borrow anything unless you have received permission. Many doozies can be prevented if you follow this simple tip.

4. Choose your battles wisely. I've seen siblings almost start World War III over the dumbest things: "But Mom, he keeps staring at me!" "Don't you dare cross this line!" (followed by one kid poking her pinkie across the imaginary line). "But I was thinking about watching *Seinfeld,* so change the channel!" Mature teenagers learn to avoid senseless battles.

5. Keep your parents out of it. Before running to your parents over every skirmish, try to work it out with your brother or sister. Consult your parents only when you both agree to do so because you can't reach an agreement any other way. This will not only help you get along better with your brothers and sisters; it will also save your parents' money in Pepto Bismol bills.

6. Treat your brothers and sisters like you would treat Jesus. Jesus told us that as we treat others, so we treat Him. When we start looking at our siblings as Christ, it changes our perspective—and how we deal with them.

7. Pray for your brothers and sisters. Prayer connects you to divine power that can help you overcome conflicts that otherwise seem impossible. It also purifies you and makes you easier to get along with.

"MOST IMPORTANT OF ALL, CONTINUE TO SHOW DEEP LOVE FOR EACH OTHER, FOR LOVE MAKES UP FOR MANY OF YOUR FAULTS" (1 PETER 4:8, TLB).

GLORIA HALLELUJAH AND A BOW TIE BEATING

It promised to be the social extravaganza of the century: my senior year prom. I splurged in preparation: a new tuxedo from Neiman-Marcus; an aqua silk bow tie from J. C. Penney; and a bottle of Jovan Musk from K Mart (a blue light special—lucky for me at that point!).

The only thing missing was a date. But how hard could that be for a senior?

I figured it was time to go for broke—Gloria. She flashed the stunning features of an LA model. Swirled blond hair. Flawless complexion. Teeth like those of the star of an Ultra Brite commercial. She was the perfect complement to my formal attire.

The invitation was impeccable. Using a quill, I sketched the invitation in Old English on a scroll of parchment. For seven hours I meticulously crafted every letter.

A fifteenth-century scribe personally delivered the invitation. The only question in my mind was whether she could wait until the next day to accept.

But she did wait until the next day. And another day. And still another day. Alas, the "Fine Damsel of Education Estates" finally did respond to my missive. Her answer came on a ripped piece of lined notebook paper with a message scribbled in pencil: "Dear Karl, I can't go with you to the prom. Your friend, Gloria."

Not stationery—lined notebook paper.

Not a fountain pen—a pencil.

Not "Love, Gloria"—"Your friend [at that point, "friend" was pushing it], Gloria."

To this day, when I hear the words "Gloria Hallelujah" I have an urge to pummel someone with my aqua bow tie. To my friends I brushed off the rejection by claiming Gloria didn't shave or shower, and I didn't want to date a good friend anyway. But to me I felt the sting of rejection and shared it with the only Friend I trusted not to reject me again.

"THERE ARE 'FRIENDS' WHO PRETEND TO BE FRIENDS, BUT
THERE IS A FRIEND WHO STICKS CLOSER THAN
A BROTHER" (PROV. 18:24, TLB).

THE FIVE QUALITIES GIRLS WANT IN A BOYFRIEND

Guys, are you tired of hanging around school programs, the shopping mall, church functions, and other "meet markets" looking for a girlfriend? Would you like to be a better boyfriend? If so, pay close attention to what the average girl is looking for in a guy. Here is my list of the top five qualities girls want.

1. Sensitivity. Girls find themselves attracted to guys who can sense their needs and feelings. Unfortunately, many guys are as sensitive as a Brillo pad. Driven by bubbling hormones, they think mostly of themselves. Girls like guys who interact well in places other than in front of a mirror.

2. Responsibility. Girls like guys who know where they're going and are responsible. Irresponsible guys ("Like let's play Nintendo for the seventeenth game in a row, dude!") are a turn-off.

3. Honesty. Honesty builds trust. As one girl told me: "Getting involved in a relationship without trust is like putting your money in a bank that is not insured."

4. Humor. My wife and I met on a blind date and hit the status of "a serious thing" shortly thereafter. During the first week

71

of constantly being together, I spared no expense in taking her to the nicest places in town. I sported a new wardrobe. I carried her books and opened the car door. I treated her like Princess Di. Ten years later, as I read in her diary of our first dates together, I was shocked she never mentioned the exquisite restaurants or the snappy clothes or the polite behavior. All she wrote was "This guy is hilarious. All we do when we're together is laugh." That's it. Often girls are more impressed with a quick wit than a colossal wallet.

5. Commitment to Christ. Girls intuitively understand that a man of God is more likely to be conscientious. And that quality is very enticing to many of them.

"SINCE YOU HAVE BEEN CHOSEN BY GOD . . . , YOU SHOULD PRACTICE TENDERHEARTED MERCY AND KINDNESS TO OTHERS. DON'T WORRY ABOUT MAKING A GOOD IMPRESSION ON THEM BUT BE READY TO SUFFER QUIETLY AND PATIENTLY. BE GENTLE AND READY TO FORGIVE" (COL. 3:12, 13, TLB).

THE FIVE QUALITIES GUYS WANT IN A GIRLFRIEND

Girls, ever wondered what qualities guys are looking for in a girlfriend? Here are my top five.

1. Honesty. Little lies will get you dropped faster than a sparking firecracker. Guys like girls who are straightforward and trustworthy. Don't lead a guy on if you're being dishonest. Girls who humiliate guys in that way are as appealing as moldy cheese. Be honest.

2. Attractiveness. I heard a girl complain, "I'm supposed to be Madonna, Dolly Parton, Paula Abdul, and Betty Crocker all in one—and all I really am is Betty Crocker."

Call it chauvinistic and shallow, but the typical guy wants an attractive girlfriend. Strive to make yourself attractive. Be cautious, however, because most guys are equally as turned off with girls who primp as much as they breathe. Don't be overly obsessed with how you look. Be yourself, and guys will find you attractive.

3. Sexual purity. The same guy who pushes you to compromise sexually is subconsciously hoping you will say no. A guy wants a girlfriend who is sexually pure. Your boyfriend will respect you more—regardless of what he might say.

4. Appreciation. Guys like girls who can express compliments to them. Don't be afraid to show appreciation to your boyfriend. My hunch is your appreciation will be a boomerang and return to you in enjoyable ways.

5. Commitment to Christ. A non-Christian friend once confided in me: "I was flirting with a chick at the pub one night when the disgust of this woman hit me. I've been known to use sleazeballs, but I'd never marry one. It was then that I realized I need to change and become the kind of person I want to attract. The girls I admire most go to your church."

Guys like girls who are committed to Christ. This quality is like flashing police lights on a dark night—you can't ignore it.

"BE KIND TO EACH OTHER, TENDERHEARTED, FORGIVING ONE ANOTHER, JUST AS GOD HAS FORGIVEN YOU BECAUSE YOU BELONG TO CHRIST" (EPH. 4:32, TLB).

Succeeding in the Tough Battles

4

BLOODY COMPROMISE

Radio personality Paul Harvey tells of how an Eskimo kills a wolf. The account offers insight into how compromising our standards can destroy us.

"First," Harvey says, "the Eskimo coats his knife blade with animal blood and allows it to freeze. Then he adds another layer of blood, and another, until frozen blood has completely concealed the blade.

"Next the hunter fixes his knife in the ground, with the blade pointing up. When a wolf follows his sensitive nose to the source of the scent and discovers the bait, he licks it, tasting the fresh frozen blood. He begins to lick faster, lapping the blade until it has bared the keen edge. Feverishly now, the wolf licks the blade harder and harder in the Arctic night. So great becomes his craving for blood that the wolf does not notice the razor-sharp sting of the naked blade on his own tongue, nor does he recognize the instant at which his own warm blood has begun to satisfy his insatiable thirst. His carnivorous appetite just craves more—until the dawn finds him dead in the snow."

Satan candy-coats sin so that it is as enticing as blood to a wolf. And as deadly.

"BE SELF-CONTROLLED AND ALERT. YOUR ENEMY THE DEVIL PROWLS AROUND LIKE A ROARING LION LOOKING FOR SOMEONE TO DEVOUR" (1 PETER 5:8).

WHAT IS SIN?

Is it a sin to eat a chocolate-chip cookie?
 Is it a sin to eat 19 chocolate-chip cookies at one time?
 Is it a sin to go to a movie?
 Is it a sin to dance?
 Is it a sin to go to a Snoop Doggy Dogg concert?
 Is it a sin to wear a miniskirt?
 What is sin?
 We tend to define "sin" in terms of behavior, thinking of it as behaving in a bad manner. Thus we view sin as something wrong we do. Consequently, Christianity becomes a list of good behaviors to follow and bad behaviors to avoid. The following poem describes this type of Christianity:

> "My mother taught me not to smoke; I don't.
> Or listen to a naughty joke; I don't.
> Wild men have wine, women, and song; I don't.
> To stay out late is very wrong; I don't.
> I kiss no girls, not even one,
> I do not know how it is done.
> You must not think I have much fun; I don't."

While we may define sin in terms of behavior that we should and shouldn't do, God uses a different model. His model is relational rather than behavioral—that is, it concentrates on a special relationship rather than what we do.

Remember the story of the prodigal son? Both sons defined sin as a bad behavior. And both of them approached the father while defining sin as the bad behavior of squandering the father's money on prostitutes and wild living.

The father, however, held to a different model of sin. His only concern was restoring the son back to the family. He clothes his son in a robe and puts the family ring back on his finger. To the father, sin is not a bad behavior. It is a broken relationship. His concern is restoring and healing that relationship.

What, then, is sin? Anything that destroys your friendship with God.

> "BUT THE FATHER SAID TO HIS SERVANTS, 'QUICK! BRING THE BEST ROBE AND PUT IT ON HIM. PUT A RING ON HIS FINGER AND SANDALS ON HIS FEET. BRING THE FATTENED CALF AND KILL IT. LET'S HAVE A FEAST AND CELEBRATE. FOR THIS SON OF MINE WAS DEAD AND IS ALIVE AGAIN; HE WAS LOST AND IS FOUND.' SO THEY BEGAN TO CELEBRATE" (LUKE 15:22-24).

SEX

PRACTICING SAFE SEX—PART 1

"Arrrrrrrrseeeeeniiiiiiiiiioooooooo Haaaaalllllll!" the announcer bellowed.

The former talk show host strutted to center stage. The band blasted. The dog pound barked. And Arsenio went to work.

"Good evening. I'm Arsenio Hall. Thank you. Thank you. I learned an interesting scientific fact today," he said as he flashed his patented smirk. "No kidding. I read—I don't know if it's true or not—but I read that individual slugs have the capacity to reproduce within themselves." The audience giggled, as if teetering on the edge of uproar.

"No kidding. One slug has the genetic capability to reproduce a baby slug—independent of any external help." He paused momentarily before he delivered the punch line. "Wow! Now, *that's* safe sex!"

OK, everyone's talking about it. So what is "safe sex"?

The world's definition: Safe sex is using precaution so you don't get diseases such as AIDS, gonorrhea, or syphilis. Whoever the partner or whatever the relationship (boy, girl, married, single), it doesn't matter as long as you don't get diseased. That's safe sex.

But God's definition is different: safe sex is using precaution so you don't even think of sexual relations outside the context of marriage. No exceptions. And had we followed God's guidelines for safe sex, we wouldn't know what venereal disease is. Now, *that's* safe sex.

"IT IS GOD'S WILL THAT YOU SHOULD . . . AVOID SEXUAL IMMORALITY; THAT EACH OF YOU SHOULD LEARN TO CONTROL HIS OWN BODY IN A WAY THAT IS HOLY AND HONORABLE, NOT IN PASSIONATE LUST LIKE THE HEATHEN, WHO DO NOT KNOW GOD" (1 THESS. 4:3-5).

PRACTICING SAFE SEX—PART 2

God not only tells us to practice safe sex, He shows us *how*. He tells us how to cope with sexual temptations. Pornography, premarital sex, masturbation, sexual fantasies—whatever your struggle, you can escape.

How? By applying four lessons from the story of Joseph. Just remember the acronym "SAFE."

Lesson 1: "S"AFE—Set Standards

"Now Joseph was well-built and handsome, and after a while his master's wife took notice of Joseph and said, 'Come to bed with me.' But he refused. 'With me in charge,' he told her, 'my master does not concern himself with anything in the house. . . . My master has withheld nothing from me except you, because you are his wife. How then could I do such a wicked thing and sin against God?'" (Gen. 39:6-9).

As soon as Potiphar's wife attempted to seduce Joseph, he had an answer. He had established his standards before he faced the sexual temptation.

Christ faced temptation in the same way. When Satan confronted Him in the wilderness, He had an immediate answer:

"It is written."

So you want to resist sexual temptation? Don't wait to make decisions until you are in the heat of battle (or lust). Set standards ahead of time so when you are tempted you already know your response.

If *you* fail to establish your standards, someone else will.

Lesson 2: S"A"FE—Avoid

"And though she spoke to Joseph day after day, he refused to go to bed with her *or even to be with her*" (verse 10).

Andy was an alcoholic. He paid dearly for his alcoholic addiction: he lost his law firm, his family, his life savings, and his self-esteem. On New Year's Day 1994 Andy decided to stop drinking. Excited about his New Year's resolution, he dashed to his favorite tavern, Buzz Inn, to share his resolutions with his old boozing buddies. He wouldn't drink, just visit.

No sooner had Andy entered the tavern than he was drinking again. You don't fight alcoholism in a bar.

Shirley was, shall we say, a bit wide for her height. Her thighs lived in separate zip codes. One evening while munching on her third Oh Henry! candy bar, she decided she'd lose 300 pounds. Her "diet" went well—until she went to work the following day at Martin's Bakery.

You don't fight the temptation to eat by hanging around a bakery.

You don't fight the temptation to drink by going to a party at which they're serving wine coolers.

You don't fight the temptation of sex at make-out mountain.

You don't fight lust by watching suggestive movies.

You don't fight sexual fantasizing by reading *Playboy*.

Avoid situations in which you know you'll be tempted. Joseph refused even to be around Potiphar's wife because he knew of the temptation.

Practicing SAFE Sex—Part 3

How can you overcome sexual temptations? Our lessons from Joseph continue.

Lesson 3: SA"F"E—Flee

"One day he went into the house to attend to his duties, and none of the household servants was inside. She caught him by his cloak and said, 'Come to bed with me.' But he left his cloak in her hand and *ran out of the house*" (verses 11, 12).

Tom and Jennifer were sophomores at Monroe High School. In the first month of school their casual acquaintance blossomed into a serious relationship. One lazy Sunday afternoon Jennifer's phone rang. "Hello," she answered.

"Hi, Jen! You want to come over?"

"Sure," she replied.

When she entered Tom's house, something didn't seem right. The drapes were pulled closed. The lights were off. The eerie atmosphere put Jennifer on edge. "Where are your folks?" she demanded.

"Oh, they're out of town for the weekend."

"How come it's so dark in here?"

"Relax, Jennifer," Tom whispered as he gently kissed her forehead. His kisses slid down her cheek. And her neck.

"What are you doing?" she demanded.

"Lighten up, Jennifer. It's not like we're weird or anything. You're probably the only virgin in high school. If you really love me, you'll trust . . ."

Jennifer didn't argue. She didn't try to reason with him. Instead, she dashed out the door like a greyhound after a rabbit.

The third lesson in safe sex is to flee. If you find you're in a situation in which you know you'll be tempted, do as Joseph did—get out of there!

Lesson 4: SAF"E"—Expect Punishment

"When his master heard the story his wife told him, saying,

'This is how your slave treated me,' he burned with anger. Joseph's master took him and put him in prison, the place where the king's prisoners were confined" (verses 19, 20).

It started out to be an evening of meaningless chatter with the guys. I started to squirm, however, when a couple of them started to describe in graphic detail their sexual exploits.

"Hey, Haffner, what about you?" Ron inquired. I felt the blood surging to my head.

"Well, I, ah, um . . ."

"Let's hear it, pretty boy," Todd mocked.

"Well, to, um, be honest, I've decided to save myself, um, ah, until I'm, ah, married," I mumbled as I gazed downward.

The group exploded in laughter. From that evening on, those guys called me "the virgin boy."

It is not popular to exercise God's plan of safe sex. Expect to be punished. But remember, Joseph also got punished. In the end, however, he was richly rewarded for refusing to compromise God's plan for safe sex.

Get the Picture?

Last spring I took my annual pilgrimage to the tulip fields in Mount Vernon, Washington. Crimsons and yellows and purples splashed across the land as far as I could see. The brilliant display of color flooded my senses. I was soaking in the wonder when a little boy dashed in front of me. His tiny fist clutching a brochure, he exclaimed, "Look, Mommy, look! Here's a picture of a tulip."

Dumb kid, I thought, *why would you care about a picture when there's something so much better? Look at the real tulips all around you!*

Satan has splashed pictures of sex everywhere. Our culture is saturated with it. His message bombards us like bullets from a brainwashing gun: "Get all the sex you can. All kinds. Anytime. You're only young once."

Yet why should we be enticed by pictures on TV and billboards and magazines when God has something so much better?

You can keep yourself pure from this day forward. It may not be easy, but it will be rewarding. Guaranteed. Both now and in that day when we'll be made royalty just like Joseph.

THE SEXUAL ESCAPADE GONE GOOD

In Robert Schuller's book *Self-Love, the Dynamic Force of Success*, he presents this classic story. Although I read it many years ago, I have never forgotten it.

"A young man shared this story with me. 'I was bored one night and went to a neighborhood bar. I met this chick, and we started drinking. She was lonely. I was bored. I was unmarried. She was divorced. "Let's go to Las Vegas," she suggested. I looked at the hungry invitation in her sultry eyes and immediately put my glass down, paid the bartender, took her arm, and headed for the car. She snuggled warmly and hungrily close to me. We roared through the night, with visions of a hot bed in a Vegas motel. For some strange reason that I cannot explain, I was suddenly gripped by the thought that this was a pretty cheap thing for me to do. I found myself mentally torn at the sexual compulsion to "shack up" with this barfly for whom I had no respect whatsoever. At the same time, glancing at the rearview mirror, I saw my own eyes. They were the eyes of a potentially wonderful person. I was beginning to feel the disgust and self-loathing that I had known on more than one previous occasion after indulging in a depersonalizing sexual escapade. I pulled over to the shoulder of the road and stopped the car. "What are you doing?" she asked.

"'"I'm getting out," I answered abruptly. "It's your car. Go on to Vegas if you want to. I don't care what you do. I'll thumb a ride back." I slammed the door shut and watched as she angrily spun the wheels in the gravel and roared furiously away. I stood there alone in the night on a lonely stretch of desert road. Suddenly I felt 10 feet tall! I never felt so good in my life! I felt like a triumphant general returning victoriously from a proud battle. That was my moment of self-love.'"

Living a clean life morally goes hand in hand with enjoying good feelings about yourself. There is no confidence like the confidence resulting from purity!

As a pastor I see a steady stream of people who ignored God's wisdom regarding sexual purity until they were devastated. Emotionally, spiritually, relationally, and physically devastated.

Because God knows our feeling of pain, He wants to spare us from it. His wisdom and purpose in restricting sexual activity to a monogamous marriage context is to keep people from getting run over, slam-dunked, and hurt. Follow God's counsel and relish in the freedom of feeling pure!

"FLEE FROM SEXUAL IMMORALITY. ALL OTHER SINS A MAN COMMITS ARE OUTSIDE HIS BODY, BUT HE WHO SINS SEXUALLY SINS AGAINST HIS OWN BODY. DO YOU NOT KNOW THAT YOUR BODY IS A TEMPLE OF THE HOLY SPIRIT, WHO IS IN YOU, WHOM YOU HAVE RECEIVED FROM GOD? YOU ARE NOT YOUR OWN; YOU WERE BOUGHT AT A PRICE. THEREFORE HONOR GOD WITH YOUR BODY" (1 COR. 6:18-20).

DRINKING

HOW TO WIN A FREE VACATION

You can win a free vacation! Guaranteed! Addison won it, and so can you.

For Addison, it included free escort service, accommodations, and meals. He didn't have to buy a raffle ticket or enter a drawing. Winning was as easy as driving . . . drunk.

"Really, Officer," Addison pleaded as the policeman shoved him into the back seat. "All I had was two, maybe three, wine coolers. But I'm not drunk." His dizzying mind swirled faster than the dancing red lights on top of the escort car. The chauffeur whisked him straight to the motel.

The motel was conveniently located in the downtown district. The receptionist at the front desk showered Addison with personalized service at check-in. She took his fingerprints, snapped his picture, gave him a breath test, asked him enough questions to complete a four-page report, then offered him the use of a telephone—for one call. Gulping, Addison then called home. When his father heard, he cursed and hung up.

Addison received a mattress cover and a thin blanket, and was led to his room. Twenty-six other people had won the same vacation (including one male prostitute who couldn't stop glancing at Addison). Since Addison was the newcomer, his bunk was conveniently located by the toilet. He had a nice view—and smell—of the relief efforts. Before the night was over, two cellmates harassed "the new pretty boy" by cramming chewing gum in his ear. He dared not sleep.

As for the free meals, breakfast was a sausage, an egg, a piece of bread, and water. After eating, Addison returned to his bunk to stare at the white walls. He had lots of time to think about what he would do the next time someone offered him a wine cooler.

In spite of his miserable vacation, however, it could have been worse. Addison might have won a free trip to the other facility on the east side of town. It's called the morgue.

"DO NOT GET DRUNK ON WINE, WHICH LEADS TO DEBAUCHERY.
INSTEAD, BE FILLED WITH THE SPIRIT" (EPH. 5:18).

DRUGS

CALL TO WORSHIP

I can make an hour of boring church seem like two minutes of ecstasy," Leslie smirked.

"Right!" I quipped. "I don't think my dad's sermons will ever seem like two minutes."

"You don't know what I know," Leslie insisted. "You wanna enjoy the sermon today?"

"Yeah, but I don't—"

"Then come with me to the van."

Leslie sauntered off like a college kid in a grade school. Somehow he was always in control. His style dripped with suaveness. It was difficult not to follow him.

I hoisted myself up to the passenger seat. "Did you get new mags on your rig?" I questioned.

"Yeah! Lookin' sweet, don't you think?"

"I like 'em."

"I'm finally getting this baby the way I want it. You wouldn't believe the chicks who give me the stares now!"

The van was definitely a head-turner. The $4,000 paint job advertised correctly: "The Rollin' Fantasy."

I relaxed in the cushy passenger's seat as we cruised past the church. The pulsating beat of Guns 'N' Roses pounded just a little faster than my heartbeat. I stared at the dancing lights on the equalizer. The stereo alone resembled the cockpit of a 747.

"Where we going, anyway?" I ventured.

"We're here," Leslie announced as he turned into Mill Creek Park.

"What's here?"

"We're getting ready for church," he replied with a grin. "Think of it as the 'call to worship.'"

Leslie looked in all directions. Secretively, he pulled a Baggie from the glove box. It looked like a pouch of oregano.

"Ever tried this stuff?" he quizzed.

"Yeah. On pizza."

Leslie giggled as if anticipating a giddy sensation. "You do know what this is, don't you?" he asked as he wrapped the weed in cigarette paper.

"Um, ah, yeah," I assured him.

Clouds of sweet reefer wafted in the van. My throbbing mind raced with the blaring music. Leslie sucked the joint and passed it to me. "Wanna hit?"

I put it to my lips and sucked. Tentatively. Cautiously. I was careful not to swallow the smoke.

The next 15 minutes were a blur. Then Leslie announced abruptly, "We gotta get you back to church. I don't wanna keep the PK from hearing Daddy preach."

The service didn't race by as I'd hoped. Questions echoed in my thick mind. Guilt clung to me like a sticky spider's web. Confusion boiled within me. Somehow I both idolized and detested Leslie.

A few weeks later my thoughts about his lifestyle changed forever. It was a Friday evening when my mother answered the phone. "Hello . . . No, he's not . . . Yes, it is . . . Oh, my lands . . . You're kidding . . . OK." Click. Mom stood in shock.

"What happened?" I asked.

"Huh?" Mom snapped to reality. "Um, ah, it's about Leslie. I guess he was in an accident. They're not sure if he's going to make it."

That evening my parents made a rare exception to the rule of no television on Friday night. We stared at the anchorman as he reported: "Four people were killed this evening when a Chevy van collided with a Volkswagen Rabbit on Highway 529. Police say the driver of the van, 18-year-old Leslie Banks, was traveling in excess of 100 miles per hour when his vehicle careened out of control into oncoming traffic. Banks is the only survivor and is listed in critical condition at the Ashville Medical Center. Police report Banks was going to the George Washington High football game and was legally drunk at the time of the accident."

The following afternoon I accompanied my father on his pastoral visits. One of his stops was the hospital.

We walked through the sterile hallways of CCU, then tiptoed into room 347. Mylar balloons and a vase of carnations splashed a dab of cheer in the white chamber. Computers beeped on a dozen monitors. Leslie's mom snoozed quietly in the corner.

I stared at Leslie. He resembled a paralyzed mummy. Tubes snaked from high-tech equipment into his arms and nose. Half of his long hair had been shaved, and his scalp exposed a crust of dried blood and stitches. His vacant stare made me wonder if he really had survived.

Dad gently touched his bandaged hand. "We need you, Leslie," he whispered. "God's with you. Be strong."

I squirmed. Although I doubted Leslie even knew we were there, I wondered what to say to him. I'd never spoken of anything spiritual to him before. He was too cool for God stuff. And yet nothing else seemed appropriate.

"Um, ah, Leslie," I stammered, "um, I'll be, ah, praying for you."

Leslie blinked as if trying to respond. A tear trickled from his eye. He blinked again.

"Hang in there, buddy," I encouraged. "I'll be praying for you."

"BUT EACH ONE IS TEMPTED WHEN, BY HIS OWN EVIL DESIRE, HE IS DRAGGED AWAY AND ENTICED. THEN, AFTER DESIRE HAS CONCEIVED, IT GIVES BIRTH TO SIN; AND SIN, WHEN IT IS FULL-GROWN, GIVES BIRTH TO DEATH" (JAMES 1:14, 15).

PEER PRESSURE

BELIEVE IT OR NOT

Circle the longest line in chart 1:

CHART 1

> **A.** _____
> **B.** ____
> **C.** ___

Psychologist Ruth W. Berenda and her associates administered this identical test to a group of teenagers. Seventy-five percent of the students claimed line A was longest.

Did you circle the right line? If not, let's try it again. Circle the
longest line in chart 2:

CHART 2

> **A.** _____
> **B.** ___
> **C.** _____

According to the study, 75 percent of the students claimed
line B was longest.

You would agree, wouldn't you? Or not?

Why would most kids vote for line B as the longest if it wasn't?
Let's try it one more time in chart 3:

CHART 3

> **A.** ____
> **B.** _____
> **C.** ___

The majority voted for line A. Did you finally get this one right?

When they administered this test, the psychologists were
studying how teenagers handle peer pressure. The plan was easy.
They ushered 10 young people into a testing room and instructed

each group to raise their hands when the leader pointed to the longest line on each of three charts.

But unbeknown to one person in the group, the other nine in the room had been told prior to the experiment to ignore the instruction to vote for the longest line and instead choose the second-longest line.

The psychologists were trying to determine how one person would react when surrounded by a large number of people who obviously voted against the truth.

Here's what happened: "The experiment began with nine teenagers voting for the wrong line. The stooge would typically glance around, frown in confusion, and slip his hand up with the group. The instructions were repeated, and the next card was raised. Time after time, the self-conscious stooge would sit there saying a short line is longer than a long line simply because that person lacked the courage to challenge the group. This remarkable conformity occurred in about 75 percent of cases, and was true of small children and high school students as well. Berenda concluded that 'Some people would rather be president than right,' which is certainly an accurate assessment."*

It's one thing to study peer pressure in a clinical setting. Things are safe. Controlled. Under the watchful eye of a professional doctor.

It's another thing, however, to grow up in a world that screams, "The second-longest line is really the longest!"

"A beer now and then can't hurt you. Look at all the kids who prove it."

"There's nothing wrong with sex outside marriage. Everyone knows that!"

"Everybody cheats a little bit in class."

Have the guts to vote against the crowd. The majority can be dead wrong.

"DO NOT CONFORM ANY LONGER TO THE PATTERN OF THIS
WORLD, BUT BE TRANSFORMED BY THE RENEWING OF
YOUR MIND" (ROM. 12:2).

*James Dobson, *Hide and Seek* (Old Tappan, N.J.: Fleming H. Revell Co., 1979), pp. 126, 127.

Spiritual Success

God

The Higher Power

One of the benefits of living in Seattle is the breathtaking view of Mount Rainier. Whenever it's not raining around here (both days a year) I gaze at the mountain and am reminded of the fascinating story of the two men who first climbed the 14,410-foot monster.

In the late nineteenth century two pioneers became obsessed with conquering it. They sought help from a local Indian guide, who informed them that his people considered it sacrilegious to climb Mount Rainier. He described God's home in the lake of fire at the crown and that no Indian would violate its sanctity by treading upon it.

The climbers offered more and more money, until eventually one guide sold out. Although the guide tried to misdirect them, the men were determined. Near the pinnacle, the guide said, "I am forbidden to go any higher. From here on you must go on alone." Bravely the men persevered, determined to conquer the mountain. They did. They took pictures. They planted a flag. They won!

Chalk up another victory for humanity.

While I admire their resolve, at a deeper, more profound level I am disturbed by their violation of a sacred trust—their conquering for human beings what had previously been reserved for God.

That's the problem with human achievement. We elevate humanity and diminish God. When Samuel F. B. Morse invented the telegraph more than 100 years ago, his first words sent by wire were "What hath God wrought!" But when Neil Armstrong stepped onto the moon in 1969, he said, "That's one small step for a man, one giant leap for mankind." Note who gets the credit in the twentieth century.

Wristwatch TVs, space travel, virtual reality, cyberspace—

technology is the enemy of reverence because it celebrates human accomplishments. It is idol worship, with humans being the idol. This is futile, however, because it can never lift us beyond ourselves. And within every human soul is a craving to be drawn out of ourselves and filled with reverence for our holy God.

No matter how much we accomplish, no matter how sophisticated our machines, we would shudder to think that human beings are ultimately in charge. As Gerald Kennedy said: "It takes more credulity to accept the atheistic position than most men can muster." The human spirit craves to cry out with the psalmist: "When I consider your heavens, the work of your fingers, the moon and the stars, which you have set in place, what is man that you are mindful of him, the son of man that you care for him?" (Ps. 8:3, 4).

Consider these two examples:

First, the Zoo

When you visit the zoo, what animals would you tend to visit most? My guess is that near the top of your list you put tigers and lions and elephants. Why? I suspect we find a calming reassurance at seeing creatures stronger and larger than ourselves. It is both humbling and comforting to be reminded we are not the ultimate power. Our souls are starved for that sense of wonder, that encounter with grandeur that helps us see our place in the universe.

Second, the Storm

Picture an icy, windy snowstorm. If you are in your car, driving on slippery, dangerous roads, you probably don't enjoy the storm. But if you are curled in front of a fire watching the snowflakes fall, the storm is therapeutic.

There's something fun about storms if we aren't threatened by them, isn't there? Isn't it a pleasant feeling to be overwhelmed by the power of nature so long as you are safe and protected?

When we reach our own limits, it is comforting to know we can turn to a Power greater than ourselves. Even atheists crave this need. In the words of Charles Locke: "Every effort to prove there is no God is in itself an effort to reach for God."

"THE HEAVENS DECLARE THE GLORY OF GOD; THE SKIES PROCLAIM THE WORK OF HIS HANDS" (PS. 19:1).

A FATHER'S PASSION

S itting in the Columbus, Ohio, airport, I was practicing my primary spiritual gift—eavesdropping. Close by, a conversation between a father and his son (who I guessed was 4 or 5) carried to me loud and clear.

"Wooooowie Voom! Daddy! Look at that one," the boy marveled, pointing at a jet taxiing on the tarmac. "Whoa! Look at that one, Daddy!" he gleamed, pointing the opposite direction at a DC-10.

The son paused for a moment, then said, "Daddy, when I be growed up, more than anything in the world I want to drive one of those jets. Can I, Daddy? Please, Daddy?"

"Sure, son, you can be a pilot if you want. You'll have to read a lot of books."

"I will, Daddy. Because more than anything I want to be jet driver when I be a grown-up."

The boy kept gawking at the airplanes, then looked to his father and asked, "Daddy, when you were my age, what did you want to grow up to be?"

I loved the father's answer. His response sent me scrambling through my luggage to record it in my journal.

The father looked at his son and said, "When I was your age, more than anything in the world I wanted to grow up to become your daddy."

Our heavenly Father responds in the same tender way to us. His deepest desire is to be our Father. To Him we are most important.

His feelings about us have nothing to do with what we do or how we behave. His love is not conditional on whether or not we smoke dope. Or go to church. Or sass our parents. His love is absolutely unconditional. God pays no attention to the external righteousness meters we are so obsessed with. His passion is for the heart.

Samuel put it this way: "The Lord does not look at the things man looks at. Man looks at the outward appearance, but the Lord looks at the heart" (1 Sam. 16:7). We are God's highest priority simply because we are His children.

God's Word

The Writing on the Walls

The prince of Grenada, an heir to the Spanish crown, was sentenced to life in solitary confinement in Madrid's ancient prison called the "Place of the Skull." The place had earned its name well. Everyone knew that once you were in, you would never come out alive. The prince received one book to read during the entire time—the Bible. With only one book to choose, he read it hundreds and hundreds of times.

After 33 years of imprisonment, he died. When they cleaned out his cell, they found some notes he had written using nails to etch the soft stone of the prison walls. His notations were of this sort: Psalm 118:8 is the middle verse of the Bible; the ninth verse of the eighth chapter of Esther is the longest verse in the Bible; no word or name of more than six syllables can be found in the Bible.

When Scot Udell commented on these notes in *Psychology Today*, he noted the peculiarity of a person who spent 33 years of his life studying what some have described as the greatest book of all time, yet could only glean trivia. From all we know, he never made any religious or spiritual commitment to Christ, but he became an expert at Bible trivia.*

How sad. How tragic. How common.

Some see the Bible as a history book. To others it is a collection of inspiring stories. Many dismiss it as a fairy tale.

---

* Reprinted from *Hot Illustrations for Youth Talks*, copyright 1994 by Youth Specialties, Inc., 1224 Greenfield Dr., El Cajon, CA 92021. Used by permission.

And then there are those who take the Bible for what it claims to be: God's Word. These believers understand the dynamic power of Scripture. They view it as the source of lasting change. Long-term transformation. Everlasting life. It is the word direct from our holy God.

Suppose you were locked up for 33 years with nothing to read except the Bible. What would you write on the walls of your cell?

"FOR PROPHECY NEVER HAD ITS ORIGIN IN THE WILL OF MAN, BUT MEN SPOKE FROM GOD AS THEY WERE CARRIED ALONG BY THE HOLY SPIRIT" (2 PETER 1:21).

SALVATION

FACTS THAT MATTER

I'm too smart to get suckered into that marketing ploy. Really. At least I like to think so.

After all, I know why savvy managers place the *TV Guide*, gum, fingernail clippers, and batteries at the checkout stand. But who would be so impulsive as to actually buy the unwanted, unnecessary junk?

Me.

I couldn't resist. The title of the book displayed next to the *National Enquirer* captured my attention. So I fell for the oldest marketing scam around and tossed it into my cart, next to the artichokes. And for $5.95, it was a worthwhile investment.

The title? *Facts That Matter! Everything You Need to Know About Everything.* Since I hadn't learned everything about everything yet, I figured it was a must-read. Maybe you are not yet familiar with some of these facts that matter so much:

- In a classic study of children and parents, fathers claimed they spent 15 to 20 minutes per day with their babies; they actually averaged 37.7 seconds.
- One in five teenagers is armed with a gun, a knife, or a club.
- A recent study concludes that students who regularly use stereo headphones cannot hear as well as those who do not, especially in the high-pitch range.
- Red and beige cars sell better on the resale market, with darker shades of blue also selling well.
- Seventy percent of all magazine cover models, 65 percent of all Miss Americas, and 64 percent of all female TV news anchors are blond.

The facts are intriguing, aren't they? But do they really matter, as the book title claims?

For example, it's relatively insignificant how many Miss Americas are blond. You will face no consequences if you forget that fact. On the other hand, some facts do matter. Some facts are a matter of life and death. For example:

- The number of people who have sinned and fall short of the glory of God is 100 percent.
- The number of people who will one day stand accountable before our holy God is 100 percent.
- The number of people who will live with Christ forever because they accepted His grace is 100 percent.

"ALL HAVE SINNED AND FALL SHORT OF THE GLORY OF GOD, AND ARE JUSTIFIED FREELY BY HIS GRACE THROUGH THE REDEMPTION THAT CAME BY CHRIST JESUS" (ROM. 3:23, 24).

Prayer

Does Prayer Work?

Some years ago the media reported the story of a man in Florida who sued his minister. The minister urged the congregation to be generous, assuring them that in return God would answer their prayers for prosperity. The man subsequently made a large contribution to the church, praying that God would reward him accordingly. When his business went bankrupt, he sued the minister for false preaching. (The judge threw the case out of court and instructed the man to take the sermons less literally.)

We tend to believe that for our prayers to work we should receive what we ask for. In this way God becomes a kind of Santa Claus, whom we approach with our wish list. When our wishes are denied, we wonder about the value of prayer. If we don't get what we want, does prayer really work?

Prayer is more than asking favors of God, more than a connection to gain an edge. Too often we pray for God to do the chores we are too lazy to do. How then should we pray? Consider these words:

"We cannot merely pray to You, O God, to end starvation;
For You have already given us the resources
With which to feed the entire world
If we would only use them wisely.
We cannot merely pray to You, O God,
To root out our prejudice,
For You have already given us eyes
With which to see the good in all men,
If we would only use them rightly.
We cannot merely pray to You, O God, to end disease,
For You have already given us great minds with which
To search out cures and healing,

If we would only use them constructively.
Therefore we pray to You instead, O God,
For strength, determination, and willpower
To do instead of just to pray,
To become instead of merely to wish."
—Jack Riemer, *Likrat Shabbot*

What good, then, is prayer if it's no guarantee for a future spouse or a miraculous cure or something else on our wish list? Of what value is prayer if we should do what we can rather than expecting God to do our chores for us? Why bother to pray at all?

Harold Kushner writes:
"Prayer is not a matter of coming to God with our wish list and pleading with Him to give us what we ask for. Prayer is first and foremost the experience of being in the presence of God. Whether or not we have our requests granted, whether or not we get anything to take home as a result of the encounter, we are changed by having come into the presence of God. A person who has spent an hour or two in the presence of God will be a different person for some time."*

When we discover the art of living in the presence of God, circumstances may not change, but our perspective does. Prayer helps us see that we are not alone. It enables us to define success beyond human terms. Our prayer will not be "Give me a new car because I deserve it" or "I need an A in geometry" or "Make my mother easier to live with." Rather, our prayer will be like that of the psalmist:

"BUT AS FOR ME, IT IS GOOD TO BE NEAR GOD" (PS. 73:28).

---

*Harold Kushner, *Who Needs God?* (New York: Summit Books, 1989), p. 148. Used by permission.

KEYS TO A FULFILLING PRAYER LIFE

It was a simple deal. Roxanne would give the sales talk, and I would pray. Simple.

She began her presentation. "Mrs. Olson, in just 30 minutes I'll show you how *Uncle Arthur's Bedtime Stories* and *The Bible Story* set can help you spiritually train your children . . ."

I began my prayer. *"Dear Heavenly Father, give Roxanne the words. Open Mrs. Olson's mind to see the value in . . ."* I strained to pray with my eyes open. My eyelids felt like bags of sand as Roxanne's familiar words floated like a lullaby.

"Which payment plan would work out best for you?" I jerked awake with the grace of a camel on ice skates. Quickly I sat up, scooting to my right to absorb the pool of drool that I had deposited on the sofa. Roxanne glanced in my direction with a glare that could have burned a hole through a steel safe.

"What were you doing?" she screamed after we got in the car.

"Sorry," I squirmed. "I, ah, was snoozing," I said sheepishly.

"No, you dweeb! It was worse."

"I know, I, um, was drooling."

"No!" she shouted. "Worse! For a half hour you were sprawled out on this stranger's couch *snoring!*"

I must admit that that's not the only episode when my prayer started with good intentions but ended in a nightmare. Maybe you too have struggled with prayer. If so, don't despair. Instead, use the keys Jesus gave us that unlock the treasury to effective prayers. In Matthew 6 Jesus makes three strong statements of what not to do that provide principles to a fulfilling and God-honoring prayer life.

Take a few minutes and read Matthew 6. Then read this summary.

1. Don't be hypocritical (verse 5).

Jesus despised meaningless God talk and pious-sounding clichés. Instead, He cherished simple, sincere sinners who approached him with every wart exposed.

100

"What a person is on his knees before God, that he is—and nothing more" (Robert Murray McCheyne).

2. Don't use meaningless repetition (verses 7, 8).

Evangelist Dwight L. Moody was once seized with the realization of how much God had blessed him with. Interrupting his eloquent prayer, he shouted, "Stop, God!"

What a welcome breath of spontaneity! It's a nice change from "Eternal, almighty, all-gracious Father of all life, Thy hand hath wonderfully and graciously provided allest of minest needs . . ." And on and on and on, grinding into snore city.

"The fewer words, the better prayer" (Martin Luther).

3. Don't ask for mercy from God until you show mercy to others (verses 14, 15).

Norman Vincent Peale once told a story from his childhood. When he was a boy, he found a big, black cigar, slipped into an alley, and lit up. It didn't taste good, but it made him feel very grown up . . . until he saw his father coming. Quickly he put the cigar behind his back and tried to be casual.

Desperate to divert his father's attention, Norman pointed to a billboard advertising the circus.

"Can I go, Dad? Please, let's go when it comes to town."

His father's reply taught Norman a lesson he never forgot. "Son," he said, "never make a petition while at the same time trying to hide a smoldering disobedience."

"Since the lines have been cleared between the Lord and me, the telephone has never stopped ringing" (Bernard L. Clark).

"My Mom's Dyin' "

The time? This morning, around 10:45.

The place? North Creek church, in the junior high classroom.

The topic? How God helps us deal with our problems.

The kids were more hyper than hummingbirds on speed. Ten

preteens packed into a room no larger than an oversized closet would probably challenge anyone's patience. They certainly did mine. For the craft session I fantasized about the students making necklaces of Valium and licking them all morning.

Our discussion was as conversational as the intercom system at an airport. "If your mom got cancer, how could God help you in that problem?" I probed. No one answered.

"If you got a ticket for riding your bike through a red light, how could God help you with that problem?" No response.

"Let's say your parents go through a divorce, could God help you in that situation?" A discussion with a sycamore tree would have been more scintillating. Everyone was preoccupied in personal discussions.

Until Damon spoke.

Damon sported the all-American look—blond hair in loose curls, a splash of faint freckles, a beaming smile, and a crooked clip-on tie.

"My mom"—he spoke just louder than a whisper—"*is* dyin'."

"Huh?" I asked, certain I hadn't heard right.

"My mom's dying of cancer."

Silence swallowed the room. The twitching kids froze like statues in shock. His statement catapulted our discussion into the real world.

"Um, I'm, ah, sorry to hear that," I stammered. "How long does the doctor say she'll live?"

"The doctor said less than two years. Then my brother and I will have to go live with my dad in Seattle. He's mean to us. My brother treats my mom real mean."

"Do you think that's because he's afraid when he thinks about your mom dying?" I grappled for the right words.

"I dunno," Damon said. "Maybe."

"I'm sorry," I offered again.

"Sometimes it's even funny. Like when my mom goes to the airport. The doctors stapled her lung together, so when she goes through the metal detector it always buzzes!"

"Any hope she may live?" I asked.

"Doctor says no."

The seconds seemed like hours. Finally Angela, the most disruptive kid in the class, blurted an unusual request: "Can we pray for you and your mother?"

"Good idea," I said. "I'll start, and if you don't want to pray, just tap the person next to you."

The simple prayers were more profound than the Psalms.

"God, help Damon's mother to make the cancer go away."

"Dear heavenly Father, sometimes nothing else works and You are the only one who can help. This would be one of those times."

"Dear Jesus, be with Damon."

Simple prayers. Just junior high kids and a muddled teacher presenting a real problem to a real God and asking for a real answer.

When we finished, once again I asked the class, "If your mom got cancer, how could God help you in that problem?"

"I don't know for sure," Damon offered. "But when I feel hurt and afraid, just having God around sure helps."

"SO DO NOT FEAR, FOR I AM WITH YOU; DO NOT BE DISMAYED, FOR I AM YOUR GOD. I WILL STRENGTHEN YOU AND HELP YOU; I WILL UPHOLD YOU WITH MY RIGHTEOUS RIGHT HAND" (ISA. 41:10).

DEVOTIONS

FILLING YOUR BASKET

An aged Christian grieved over her inability to remember what she read in the Bible. Because of this, she began to question the value of Bible study. *After all,* she wondered, *why bother when only moments after closing my Bible I can't recall what I read? I'm surely not changing any—I'm the same old sinner I was as a youngster.*

One typical evening she hobbled to bed, grumbling about how it was useless to read what so quickly dissolved from her mind. That night she had a dream. Standing on the bank of a beautiful stream whose crystal waters rippled over her feet, she held a loosely woven basket in her hand. By her side stood an angel in a resplendent robe who encouraged her to fill the basket with living water. Again and again she tried to fill it, but the loose mesh would not retain the water. No matter how careful she was, the water flowed out.

Disheartened, she turned away. "The basket is useless to hold water," she moaned.

Tenderly bending over her, the angel whispered, "Look inside your basket, my friend." Gazing with tear-dimmed eyes, the woman saw that the basket, once sullied and dirty, was now white as snow.

So it is with the Word of God. We may forget what we read. We may batter ourselves when our lives seem hopelessly stained with sin. We may curse in despair because our efforts to change seem futile.

"I'll never conquer pornography."

"Booze is the only way I can cope."

"I'm stuck with my violent temper forever."

As we fume in frustration, it seems that even the Bible is powerless against our fortress of sin. But Scripture rings clear: "Study to shew thyself approved unto God, a workman that needeth not to be ashamed, rightly dividing the word of truth" (2 Tim. 2:15, KJV).

That's not a popular text in a world of quick fixes and slick gimmicks. We want microwaves, not crockpots. Drive-thru, not sit-down. Quick, fast, and easy.

Today we want plastic piety, not life transformation. Perfect behavior, not pure character. Capable hands, not a clean heart.

In our world of quick fixes and slick gimmicks, God calls us to the discipline of study, to the gritty work of learning, to the real world where change is slow and difficult.

But who has time for that? I suspect the problem is not that we can't find the time for serious study, but of convincing ourselves that it is important enough to find the time. We want to believe there is an easier pathway to change.

But no shortcut exists. Only through the discipline of study do we change. For study is the way we get changed from the inside out. It transforms our thought processes. Perhaps we study a flower or a book. We see and feel it. As we do, our thought processes take on an order conforming to the order in the object. When we do this with focus and repetition, it forms ingrained habits of thought. While it takes discipline and concentration, it is well worth our most serious effort.

So keep filling your basket with the Living Water.

Sharing

The Sabbath School Report

Good morning and welcome to Sabbath School class! It hardly seems possible we're at the beginning of a new year already. I trust you had a safe and enjoyable Christmas."

"Good morning and welcome to KXOV channel 2 news. It hardly seems possible we're at the beginning of a new year already. I trust you had a safe and enjoyable Christmas."

"Before the lesson study, I think one item should take top priority."

"And now for today's top news story."

"It has been brought to my attention that our present system of recording daily lesson study has inconsistencies in it. I don't know exactly what you feel constitutes a 'daily lesson study,' but I feel it is most important that we use a uniform policy.

"Israeli forces attacked several Muslim Shiite villages in southern Lebanon today, killing an undisclosed number of innocent people. This attack occurred shortly after the Israeli Army command announced that one of its soldiers had been killed and four wounded in a clash with Lebanese guerrillas."

"If I could have the floor for just a minute, I think it's useless to discuss what 'daily lesson study' means. Isn't it obvious? You report daily lesson study if you studied every day—nothing else. Now let's discuss our lesson for today."

"In local news the Salvation Army has once again been operating its holiday soup kitchen. According to spokesman Michael Carmon, volunteers are still needed to serve an average of 125 people a day. If you or someone you know can help, call 473-4932."

"Thank you for your opinion, Mrs. Marshall, but I would like to see room for emergencies. For example, what happens if a person studies the lesson diligently every day yet something comes up and on one day she fails to study yet studies the same lesson the following day? Would she still not be able to count daily lesson study? After all, she did study the entire lesson. I think that's the critical issue. Now can we get on with our lesson?"

"Thirty-year-old Bryan Garvis was found frozen to death in an alley off Burnside Avenue at approximately 5:30 this morning. Apparently Bryan had been out all night. The temperatures this year are unusually cold, so we continue to advise people to stay inside as much as possible."

"Certainly your point is well taken, Mr. Charles, but it does leave room for legalists to take advantage of the system. What is to stop people from classifying everything as 'emergencies' and quickly skim the entire lesson Sabbath morning and count that as daily lesson study. Then anyone could . . . " "The after-Christmas shopping rush is on. Shoppers jammed into local malls today to take advantage of big savings. The national retail clothing consumer index was up a stunning 7.45 percent this holiday season."

"Hold on, Mr. Montgomery. I think we should make a rule that no time should be counted if the study occurred during the Sabbath hours. That way it would be our time we would be giving to the Lord, not the Lord's time."

"Robert Stevens was sentenced today to life imprisonment after pleading guilty to first-degree criminal sexual conduct with 11 different minors over the past six years. Stevens was well known in this community as the 'honest car dealer.' He will be in the Cullum County Jail."

"I'm sorry our time is quickly slipping by. I'm afraid we must postpone this critical issue. Before we leave, I'd like to read the Scripture for today: 'Then he will say to those on his left, "Depart from me, you who are cursed, into the eternal fire prepared for the devil and his angels. For I was hungry and you gave me nothing to eat, I was thirsty and you gave me nothing to drink, I was a stranger and you did not invite me in, I needed clothes and you did not clothe me, I was sick and in prison and you did not look after me"' [Matt. 25:41-43]. That's one of my favorite passages and indeed worth consideration. That about sums up the lesson. Thank you for your participation, and we will see you next week. Have a great day."

"That sums up our 6:00 report. Thank you for watching, and we will see you tonight at 5:00. Have a great day."

GRITTING MY TEETH

The electric chair. Sweat moistened my body as I trudged toward it. "Sit here," the attendant commanded.

I plopped in the chair awaiting the torture. I stared vacantly at the "No Smoking" sign above the doorway.

The attendant approached the switch. She flipped the lever. I felt the power surging in the chair.

"There you go, Mr. Haffner, that's about the right height," she remarked as she flipped the switch off. "Just wait here. The dentist will be with you in a minute."

"Ah, um, ah, thank . . ." The words caught in my throat like dry sunflower seeds.

Maybe I won't have any cavities this time, I thought to myself.

Reconsidering, I thought again. *Right, Karl! That's about as likely as Elizabeth Taylor celebrating her fiftieth wedding anniversary.*

I stared at the poster on the wall. It was a close-up of a grinning mouth sporting diseased gums. The teeth (the three that remained) were yellow and spotted, exhibiting the rotten banana look. The caption taunted me: "Avoid Gingivitis! Do You Floss Regularly?"

The Question

The clamor blared around me. I heard a duet with a howling kid and the buzzing drill, the "light tunes" of KLIT in the tinny speaker above me, and the gurgling miniature sink beside me.

I could already taste the experience: the sour Novocain, the bitter squeaky gloves of the dentist, and the bubble-gum-flavored fluoride treatment.

Twenty-six minutes after the secretary told me "The dentist will be with you in a minute," Dr. Johnston entered my cell. "Hi, Karl," he chirped. "We'll get you going here by doing a cleaning. Your dental hygienist today will be Jill."

Twelve minutes later Jill dashed into the room. "Hi, ah, Mr., um [after looking down at my chart], Haffner."

"Hi."

"How are you today?"

"Good," I lied.

As she curled some floss around her fingers I knew her next question. Oh, how I dreaded that question. *Please*, I thought to myself, *don't ask me "The Question." Any question but "The Question."* Guilt overwhelmed me.

"Do you floss?"

I knew she'd ask me that!

Why is it, I thought to myself, *every time I leave the dentist's office I swear to myself I'll start flossing everyday, then disregard my covenant within a week?*

"No, not usually," I confessed meekly.

"You really need to."

"I know."

"Once you get in the habit, it will be easy."

Her words echoed in my mind: "Once you get in the habit, it will be easy."

Determined

Although I left the office that day determined to start a new habit, I knew it would not be easy. And it wasn't.

The first week was torment. Even though I cheated with "sissy" floss (waxed and spearmint-flavored), I still struggled to continue my new habit. I twisted and yanked the string in my mouth during the entire 11:00 evening news.

"Flossing is so barbaric," I muttered to my wife one evening while licking my bleeding gums. "I feel like quitting this new habit kick I'm on."

"Practice what you preach," she retorted.

"What do mean?"

"You know, you're always preaching about making a commitment, then acting on that decision, not your feelings. You might never feel like flossing. But if you decide what you want to do, then act on it . . ."

"Yeah, yeah, I know." Suddenly my sermons flooded my mind—even though I'd never preached about flossing.

Cherié went to bed while I strained with my floss. Psyching myself up, I repeated in my mind, "Determine your actions, then act with determination."

In time I flossed daily without thinking about it.

The Question Returns

Then came the dreaded day—time for my annual pilgrimage to the dentist.

A new dental hygienist wearing her starchy white uniform sauntered into the room. "Hi," she said, "my name's Trisha."

She leaned over my mouth and began to poke and scratch with her mirrors and instruments. Then she exclaimed, "You sure have nice teeth."

I wanted to say thank you, but found it difficult to talk with her fingers in my mouth.

Then she asked that dreaded question, "Do you floss?"

Fingers or no fingers in my mouth, I had labored too hard to let the question go unanswered. I had earned the right to brag. "Why, of course!" I grinned. "I've flossed every day since I came here last year."

"I can sure tell," she affirmed.

I sat tall in the electric chair, almost enjoying the experience. Between reading *People* magazine and listening to Trisha, the time whizzed by.

"What do you do, Karl?" Trisha inquired.

"I'm the minister of the North Creek Seventh-day Adventist Church."

"Oh, really? I go to the Eastside Foursquare church."

"Yeah?" I replied. "I listen to your pastor's radio program every once in a while."

"I've only been saved for four months now. I go to church every week, but I sure wish I could be more consistent with my daily Bible study," she confessed. "Life gets so busy that it's easy to skip personal devotions."

"Yeah, it's hard sometimes," I agreed.

"Any suggestions on how to be more consistent with my devotions?" she inquired as she set down her tools.

"I guess just get into the habit," I remarked. "You have to make up your mind and then act on that commitment, rather than acting on whether or not you feel like having devotions."

"That makes sense," she agreed.

"Determine your actions, then act with determination," I continued. "Faith is not a chance, but a choice. You determine . . ."

I'd love to finish this story, but it's time for the 11:00 news—and flossing.

"THEN THEY WILL CALL TO ME BUT I WILL NOT ANSWER; THEY
WILL LOOK FOR ME BUT WILL NOT FIND ME. SINCE THEY
HATED KNOWLEDGE AND DID NOT CHOOSE TO FEAR
THE LORD" (PROV. 1:28, 29).

CHRIST'S STANDARD OF SUCCESS

Christ journeyed the pathway to success. But His route was not a typical one. While the world screams, "Bully your way to the top!" Christ teaches, "Humble yourself at the bottom." Jesus came from the highest pinnacle as one equal with God in order to serve the lowest of human beings. The Owner of everything became nothing. He descended into greatness.

A children's story tells of an ambitious caterpillar named Stripe, who decided to climb a different sort of mountain—a huge mountain of caterpillars, all scrambling over one another, trying to get to the top. As Stripe plunged into the pile and began his ascent, he asked, "What's at the top?" Another climber responded, "No one knows, but it must be awfully good because everybody's rushing there."

Stripe soon found that getting up the mountain was a constant struggle. He was pushed and kicked and stepped on from every direction. It was climb or be climbed upon. But Stripe disciplined himself neither to feel nor be distracted as he continued to push his way up. "Don't blame me if you don't succeed! It's a tough life. Just make up your mind," he yelled to any complainers.

Finally Stripe neared the top of this humongous mountain of caterpillars. And as he looked ahead, he saw something disturbing: a tremendous pressure and shaking were sending many at the top crashing to their deaths below.

The new knowledge made him feel terrible. The mystery of the pillar was clearing—he now knew what always must happen on the pillar. Frustration surged through him.

Just then he heard a tiny whisper from the top: "There's nothing here at all." Someone else answered, "Quiet, fool! They'll hear you down the pillar. We're where they want to be. That's what's here."

111

A strange coldness filled the caterpillar. To be so high and not be high at all. *It only looked good from the bottom.**

"YOUR ATTITUDE SHOULD BE THE SAME AS THAT OF CHRIST JESUS: WHO, BEING IN VERY NATURE GOD, DID NOT CONSIDER EQUALITY WITH GOD SOMETHING TO BE GRASPED, BUT MADE HIMSELF NOTHING, TAKING THE VERY NATURE OF A SERVANT, BEING MADE IN HUMAN LIKENESS" (PHIL. 2:5-7).

---

* Trina Paulia, *Hope for the Flowers* (Mahwah, N.J.: Paulist Press, 1978), pp. 21-24.

THE PATHWAY OF SUCCESS

In a word, our culture defines success as *up*. Claw, climb, conquer. Today success means power, spotlights, money, fame, and pleasure. The only way to get there is up. Flex your muscles of iron will. Defy the odds. Cheat. Stomp over people. Look out for yourself, because nobody else will. Up clearly is the direction of greatness.

But Christ defines success as *down*. Serve, support, sacrifice.

According to Him, success means powerlessness, anonymity, downscaling, self-abandonment, giving, and dying. The only way to get there is down. Swallow your ego. Abandon your own interests for the sake of others. Mow the elderly woman's lawn. Settle for a lower grade on your test in order to help someone else succeed. To give up is to gain. Down clearly is the direction of greatness.

Christ's life is a jolting model of downward mobility. He enters the world in a barn reeking with the stench of dung and urine. Rats scurry about. It is dank. And dark. A more humble place of birth could not be chosen.

This Baby had overlooked the worlds. Object of universal praise, He was equal with God. Now He cries. The prickly straw scratches His tender skin. He squirms helplessly.

The astonishing dimensions of Christ's descent are unfathomable. The One worthy of all worship rests in a stable; the Owner of all has no home; the King of kings chooses to be a servant.

And Christ's descent does not stop as He matures. Hanging out with the rejects, He heals lepers and embraces outcasts. He hugs the scorned and loves the unlovables.

In a world in which women were only a grade above farm animals, He searches them out and restores their dignity. A five-time divorcee. A sister at a funeral. A prostitute busted in the act of her sin. Jesus does not condemn them—He seeks only to restore and elevate.

At his death Jesus' descent is complete. He hangs on a cross, His body whip-torn flesh. His face is a mask of oozing blood and dripping spit, and His eyes puffy and swollen. A crown of thorns pierces His scalp.

Every muscle screams for relief. Spikes pulse fire through Him. Legs contort to find comfort. But there is no comfort on a cross.

From the world's perspective, the cross symbolizes foolishness. But from God's perspective, it stands for greatness. For only in sacrificing ourselves for the glory of God do we discover the pathway to joy.

"AND BEING FOUND IN APPEARANCE AS A MAN, HE HUMBLED HIMSELF AND BECAME OBEDIENT TO DEATH—EVEN DEATH ON A CROSS! THEREFORE GOD EXALTED HIM TO THE HIGHEST PLACE AND GAVE HIM THE NAME THAT IS ABOVE EVERY NAME, THAT AT THE NAME OF JESUS EVERY KNEE SHOULD BOW, IN HEAVEN AND ON EARTH AND UNDER THE EARTH, AND EVERY TONGUE CONFESS THAT JESUS CHRIST IS LORD, TO THE GLORY OF GOD THE FATHER" (PHIL. 2:8-11).

Discipline

How to Resist Temptation

An Eskimo owned two husky dogs that he had trained as fighters. As he roamed from village to village, he encouraged the locals to bet on the dogfights he staged. One of the dogs was darker than the other, so he took turns betting on either the lighter or the darker husky to win each match. Somehow he had the uncanny ability to always pick the winning dog. Consequently, he reaped enormous profits as he traveled through Alaska.

Just before he died, he finally answered the question that others had asked hundreds of times. "How did you always know which dog would win?"

At last he revealed his secret. "It was easy," he said. "The winner was always the dog I was feeding."

So it is with sin. Two natures—a sinful nature and a spiritual nature—fight within us. They are constantly battling for victory. Which nature will win? Whichever one you are feeding.

A close examination of how Jesus battled temptation reveals how He overcame sin. It wasn't by hoping temptation wouldn't happen. (Temptation is as sure as homework.) It wasn't by gritting his teeth and repeating 70 times an hour: "I won't sin." (Sin is stronger than grit.) Nor was it by pretending He could never be lured by Satan's bait. (His bait is as enticing as a pint of Ben and Jerry's Cherry Garcia ice cream).

When temptation confronted Jesus, He resisted by saying, "It is written . . ." Clearly, Jesus had been feeding His spiritual nature. He had so submerged Himself in Scripture that His spiritual nature controlled His impulses. That's how He won the battle. And that's how we can win.

So what is your battle? Anger? Alcohol? Appetite? Premarital sex? Whatever the temptation, resist by feeding your spiritual nature. Only then can God's power in you overcome sin.

"SUBMIT YOURSELVES, THEN, TO GOD. RESIST THE DEVIL, AND HE WILL FLEE FROM YOU" (JAMES 4:7).

COMMUNITY

COMMUNITY

A teenage boy in Milwaukee, Wisconsin, had cancer and was in the hospital for several weeks for chemotherapy and radiation. Consequently, he lost his hair. When he left the hospital, he felt troubled. Not about the cancer, but about the thought of returning to school with a bald head. He had already decided not to wear a wig or a cap.

When he walked into his home room, to his shock, about 50 of his classmates jumped and screamed, "Surprise! Welcome home!"

He was surprised. As he looked at his buddies he could hardly believe what he saw—all of his friends had shaved their heads!

Wouldn't it be nice to have friends so committed that they would shave their heads in order to make you feel loved and included? That's what God has called his church to be—a community of love and acceptance. A community of people who don't ignore a festering cancer, but rather sacrifice whatever is necessary in order to bring healing.

Whenever cancer appears in the body of Christ, it will result in pain and death. Such sickness must be dealt with.

When a friend is experimenting with pot, love confronts. When a buddy is practicing unsafe sex, members of God's community must challenge his behavior. When a parent is abusive, God's church should respond.

But always in love. Always with the motive of healing.

Nowhere in Scripture do we find this more dramatically illustrated than at Calvary. God chose not to ignore the cancer in the human race. But He did not punish us for having cancer, nor did He stay at home and let us fend for ourselves.

Rather, He became one of us. Fully identifying with us, He took upon Himself our cancer so that our fractured relationship with God might be restored. In short, He modeled for us the kind of community He has called us to be.

"LIVE A LIFE OF LOVE, JUST AS CHRIST LOVED US AND GAVE HIMSELF UP FOR US AS A FRAGRANT OFFERING AND SACRIFICE TO GOD." "FOR WE ARE MEMBERS OF HIS BODY" (EPH. 5:2, 30).

Success: What Does It Mean?

6

WHAT *DOES* IT MEAN TO BE SUCCESSFUL?

hilosopher Thomas Carlyle once wrote, "Let each become all that he was created capable of being." I like that as a definition of success. We are successful when we do our best with what we have. As Wynn Davis said: "Success means doing the best we can with what we have. Success is in the doing, not the getting—the trying, not the triumph."

Success, then, is not the end result, but the process. It comes in the journey, not in the trophy at the end. Let's wrap it up with a snapshot of successful people:

- Successful people enjoy peace even through difficult circumstances. Rather than complaining about the turbulence they encounter, they adapt and enjoy the ride.
- Successful people like themselves. They are thankful for their own uniqueness.
- Successful people maintain a positive outlook. They look for the good in others and usually find it.
- Successful people maintain healthy relationships. They get along with others and are comfortable in their relationship with God.
- Successful people have direction and purpose. Refusing to let peer pressure sway them, they are too focused to be sidetracked with drugs, alcohol, or anything else. They tenaciously set, focus on, and accomplish worthwhile goals.
- Successful people nurture the spiritual soul. They un-

derstand that spiritual well-being is the foundation of success.

- Successful people maintain high standards in their personal conduct. They know integrity is an essential ingredient of success, so they refuse to compromise it. Their public and private life are identical.
- Successful people get the most out of life because they put the most into it. They persevere. They work hard. Exercising courage, they give of themselves. Reaping what they sow, they enjoy the harvest.

Just for Teens

Barbie

Barbie seems to have it all until her dad's accident changes her comfortable lifestyle. Judi and her good-looking brother, Tom, help Barbie realize that happiness isn't hinged on a lot of money. By VeraLee Wiggins. Paper, 128 pages. US$5.05, Cdn$8.65.

***Insight's* Most Unforgettable Stories**

After 20 years of printing memorable stories, *Insight* pulls out its best: 60 Christian masterpieces that sweep you up in their emotive power . . . that twist unexpectedly and surprise you with sublime truth . . . that bring you smiles, tears, and flashes of self-discovery. Chris Blake, compiler. Paper, 191 pages. US$9.95, Cdn$14.45.

Just Don't Make Me Do the Dishes

Stephen becomes increasingly rebellious toward his adopted family until he finds himself in trouble at a boarding academy. There he learns something special about real love. By Sharon R. Todd. Paper, 128 pages. US$5.95, Cdn$8.65.

Let's Pick on Benjy!

The vicious dogs on Benjy's paper route are nothing compared to the kids at his new high school who tease him for being over-weight. Piper, one of the most popular girls in school, teaches him a valuable lesson about self-acceptance. By VeraLee Wiggins. Paper, 128 pages. US$5.95, Cdn$8.65.

Runaway Love

Seriously questioning her parents' judgment, Genie finds herself torn between keeping their trust and losing her one chance with Paul. Do her parents just want to ruin her fun? Or will dating Paul prove a dreadful mistake? By VeraLee Wiggins. Paper, 110 pages. US$5.95, Cdn$8.65.

Tough Guy

In this story about coping with the pressures of growing up, Trace realizes that the smart kids hang on to God. By Andy Demsky. Paper, 110 pages. US$5.95, Cdn$8.65.

More Great Stories

P.K. the Great

Through a series of adventures—and misadventures—cocky Jack discovers that the only way to be truly great is to accept the fact that he isn't the greatest—Jesus is. By Colleen Reece. Paper, 96 pages. US$5.95, Cdn$8.65.

Plain, Plain Melissa Jane

Freckle-nosed Melissa Jane longs to be beautiful. A stray puppy brings her more worry and joy than she could have dreamed possible and helps her learn something very special about beauty. By Colleen Reece. Paper, 125 pages. US$5.95, Cdn$8.65.

The Singing Room

When Brooke's parents decide to separate and her little sister needs surgery, she needs someone to talk to. Could God make a difference in her life? By Bev Ellen Clarke. Paper, 160 pages. US$5.95, Cdn$8.65.

A Summer of My Own

Nikki is enjoying her first summer away from home. And a fun-filled day at the beach almost makes her forget her secret pain until Allan mentions her father again. How could she tell him what she'd done to her dad? In this story by Bev Ellen Clarke, Nikki learns about forgiveness. Paper, 142 pages. US$5.95, Cdn$8.65.

Three Blondes in a Honda

Lynn and her sisters' troubled lives are changed when they run away and find shelter at an Adventist camp meeting. By Bobbie Montgomery. Paper, 143 pages. US$5.95, Cdn$8.65.

To order, call **1-800-765-6955,** or write to ABC Mailing Service, P.O. Box 1119, Hagerstown, MD 21741. Send check or money order. Enclose applicable sales tax and 15 percent (minimum US$2.50) for postage and handling. Prices and availability subject to change without notice. Add GST in Canada.

What'll We Do With Weird Uncle Will?

Dirk expected his home to change when his strange uncle came to live with him. But his heart? That was a different story. By VeraLee Wiggins. Paper, 109 pages. US$5.95, Cdn$8.65.

The Bucky Stone Books

by David B. Smith

1. Making Waves at Hampton Beach High

Bucky didn't get to go to academy, so he's decided to make the best of public school, and that means sharing Christ. It's going to be a pretty radical year for everyone involved!

2. Showdown at Home Plate

It's late Friday afternoon during the championship game, and every eye is on Bucky. Should he takes his turn at bat, or be true to his conviction not to play on Sabbath?

3. Outcast on the Court

Bucky has what it takes to help lead the Panthers to victory. But winning won't be easy with his fiercest opposition coming from his own coach and team.

4. Bucky's Big Break

Bucky's new job as a bank teller opens up all kinds of possibilities for his future—if he lives long enough to have one. One of his customers has a gun.

5. Bad News in Bangkok

Bucky's 9,000 miles from home, hopelessly lost on the streets of Bangkok. Somewhere in the huge city are friends he'd give anything to see again. But it will take almost a miracle to find them.

6. Bucky's Close Shave

It's the championship game of Bucky's basketball team, and two gamblers want Bucky to fix the game. They're prepared to offer $5,000. But if Bucky won't cooperate, they're prepared to do a lot more!

7. Bucky Gets Busted

Bucky's weekend plans strike out when his friend gets him

busted. The nightmare weekend starts him thinking about the importance of integrity.

Each paperback US$5.95, Cdn$8.65.
Look for others in the series coming soon.
